Behavioral Addictions

Behavioral
Addictions

Edwina Rogers

To order additional copies of this book, contact:
Xlibris
1-888-795-4274
www.Xlibris.com
Orders@Xlibris.com
748997

Contents

PART I

Behavioral Addictions

CHAPTER 1

Behavioral Addictions: An Overview

Chapter Overview

This chapter will provide a basic overview and understanding about behavioral addictions and specifically focus on the differences and similarities between behavioral addiction and other clinical issues. We will also introduce the DSM-5 diagnostic criteria and compare it to historical categorizations of this heterogeneous group of disorders. Overall, you can expect this chapter to help orient you to the various aspects of behavioral addictions.

Historical Context and DSM Revisions

Accounts of gambling and sex addictions can be found in early Roman writings, and a text on mental illness written nearly 200 years ago by Benjamin Rush also addressed "excessive sexual desires" (Sun, Ashley, & Dickson, 2012). However, because many of these behaviors represent extreme engagement in what otherwise might be an appropriate or even necessary behavior (eating, sex, exercise, for example), and because these behaviors have not fit neatly into previously established clinical categories, there is continued debate on appropriate treatment and little research despite a long history of anecdotal client experiences (Ascher, Levounis, & American Psychiatric Association, 2015). Only recently with newer technologies such as brain imaging and deeper understanding of addiction psychology are we beginning to paint a full portrait of this field. While the DSM-5 helps give some diagnostic clarity to these concerns, many of the other behavioral addictions discussed in this guide have no formal diagnosis in the DSM.

The term, Behavioral Addictions is an umbrella term to describe a variety of disorders including pyromania, kleptomania, pathological gambling, trichotillomania, compulsive shopping, Internet addiction and a growing list of other concerns. Some of these disorders seem linked with substance abuse, while others fall somewhere in the impulsive or compulsive spectrum (Rosenberg & Feder, 2014). These behaviors can also be separated into two major groups: first, those with legal implications such as gambling, Internet addiction, kleptomania, sexual addiction, pyromania, and second, more self-focused behaviors including compulsive exercising, compulsive eating, compulsive tanning and behaviors such as hair pulling and excoriation where the legal implications are less direct (Ascher et al., 2015). Though these disorders are dispersed into separate chapters in the Diagnostic and Statistical Manual of Mental Disorders, Fifth Edition (DSM-5), there are practical similarities that justify considering them as an inclusive grouping. Let's consider a brief history of how they have been categorized, with a focus on the recent DSM-5 changes.

Including Behavioral Addictions in the DSM-5

In the fourth edition of the DSM the category of impulse disorders not elsewhere classified included: pathological gambling, kleptomania, trichotillomania, pyromania, intermittent explosive disorder, and impulse control disorders not otherwise specified (APA 2000). During the 14-year revision process prior to the publishing of the DSM-5 in 2013, a number of additional disorders were suggested for inclusion with specific focus on Internet use and gaming disorder (compulsive buying, binge eating disorder, compulsive sexual behaviors, excessive tanning, and hoarding were also considered) (Association, 2013b). The revised DSM-5 chapter, "Substance-Related and Addictive Disorders," included pathological gambling disorder as the single condition in a new category on behavioral addictions. Internet gaming disorder was included in Section III of the manual, "Emerging Models and Measures," which includes a set of disorders subject to further study and potential inclusion in subsequent editions of the DSM. Much of the current research on Internet addictions is from studies done in Asian countries and further research is required before consideration of its inclusion as a formal disorder (2013). The inclusion of gambling disorder in this section was meant to reflect research findings that gambling disorder is similar to substance-related disorders in clinical expression, brain origin, comorbidity, physiology, and treatment (2013). Though many of the other behavioral addictions share similarities with substance use disorders, they were not included in this section.

Other behaviors that fall under the umbrella of behavioral addictions were assigned to different chapters of the revised DSM-5 (Association, 2013a). Binge Eating Disorder is included under the newly minted "Feeding and Eating Disorders" chapter, whereas Intermittent Explosive Disorder, Pyromania and Kleptomania are found under the category of "Disruptive, Impulse-Control, and Conduct Disorders". The chapter on "Obsessive-Compulsive and Related Disorders" includes Hoarding Disorder and Excoriation (skin picking), as well as Trichotillomania, which were moved from the classification of Impulse-Disorders Not Elsewhere Classified to this new chapter reflecting evidence that these three disorders are closely related.

Major Questions Surrounding Behavioral Addictions

Overall, the DSM-5 helps to clarify behavioral addictions, and the inclusion of pathological gambling under the category of substance abuse reflects current research in neurobiology and represents a movement towards understanding these behaviors as addictive patterns similar to substance use disorders. But many questions remain (Jon E. Grant, 2008). Are the rest of these disorders similar to substance abuse disorders? Or are they more closely linked to impulsive or compulsive disorders? Are there differences among these similar behaviors that would require the group to be split? Should we be categorizing them at all, or do we run the risk of pathologizing life-style differences and personal preferences? How do we interact with behaviorally addicted patients who defend their actions with the claims that they are simply enthusiasts? While the differences can be subtle, the resulting treatment implications for individual clients are potentially significant.

Though more research must be done, and while many unanswered questions persist, researchers are beginning to compile strong evidence that displays the genetic and neurochemical basis underlying some of these behaviors. This research, along with recognition of many of these disorders in the revised DSM, legitimizes patient concerns as worthy of investigation, careful diagnosis and proper intervention. Embarrassment and stigmatization stemming from lack of understanding or labeling these behaviors as poor judgement prevented appropriate clinical care and has reduced the focus given to these concerns.

Defining the Terms: What is a behavioral addiction?

The word addiction derives from the Latin root *addictus* which refers to a "person enslaved for debt or theft" (Sun et al., 2012). This definition, with the use of the word enslaved, captures the loss of control felt by individuals who suffer from an addiction. While not initially associated directly with excessive alcohol and drug use, the word addiction is now used predominantly in regards to that category of concerns, though the DSM itself avoids the use of "addiction" for substance use disorders (Ascher et al., 2015). In more modern terms, the American Society of Addiction Medicine defines addiction in the following manner:

> *Addiction is a primary, chronic disease of brain reward, motivation, memory and related circuitry...This is reflected in an individual pathologically pursuing reward and/or relief by substance use and other behaviors. Addiction is characterized by inability to consistently abstain, impairment in behavioral control, craving, diminished recognition of significant problems with one's behaviors and interpersonal relationships, and a dysfunctional emotional response... Without treatment or engagement in recovery activities, addiction is progressive and can result in disability or premature death (Medicine, 2011).*

To summarize, addiction is a chronic disease where an individual pursues reward or relief through substance use or other behavior with the inability to abstain consistently from the behavior despite significant consequences. Current estimates state that abuse of tobacco, alcohol and illicit drugs cost the US more than $700 billion annually in costs related to health care, crime, and lost work productivity (NIDA, 2015). These numbers do not include the behavioral addictions, and even just pathological gambling disorder alone may increase this number dramatically.

Similar to a general addiction, a behavioral addiction is characterized by the obsession or compulsion to engage in a particular behavior, where the patient lacks the self-control to abstain from the behavior despite negative consequences. Consider the following case study of a patient whose initial concerns are summarized as follows:

Gary at the Casino: A Case Study

Gary, 26, found himself struggling to make ends meet after the birth of his second child and after he was passed over for a promotion at work. One night while driving home he notices a sign for a local casino and stops in. He feels thrilled after being treated like a king, with free drinks and attention, and leaves after winning $200. Soon visiting the casino becomes a nightly stop on his way home from work and he even begins cutting his work hours short to spend more time at the casino. His already-stressed wife becomes increasingly suspicious as she notices his unexplained changes in schedule and increasingly high withdrawals from their savings account and suspects that he is cheating on her. Though Garry attempts to reduce his gambling, increasing debt drives him to the casino more often in an attempt to erase his mistakes, and intermittent winnings reinforce his belief that he can solve his problems at the roulette table. A year later Garry's wife moves out, he loses custody of his children along with his job, as his employer becomes increasingly frustrated by him leaving early, and he is in significant, paralyzing debt. It is then that he comes to seek treatment for his self-identified gambling problems.

Gary's Diagnosis

Under the DSM-5 it would be possible to diagnose Garry with pathological gambling addiction (Association, 2013b). It is clear to see that Garry quickly lost control of his gambling and continued despite harrowing consequences in his primary relationships and his ability to continue working, matching the definition for addiction and the more specific context of a behavioral addiction. Understanding Garry's issues will help the clinician decide on the best treatment to support him in moving forward and managing the consequences of his behavior. We will discuss treatment options in more detail later, but emphasize the point that proper diagnosis has real world implications for effective treatment.

Behavioral Addiction's Core Qualities

Next, let's consider a more specific definition of behavioral addictions. Grant (2008) writes that behavioral addictions (he refers to the category broadly as impulse control disorders as he is writing prior to the 2013 release of the DSM-5) share the following core qualities:

1. Repetitive or compulsive engagement in a behavior despite adverse consequences
2. Diminished control over the problematic behavior
3. An appetitive urge, or craving state prior to engagement in the problematic behavior, and
4. A hedonic quality during the performance of the problematic behavior (p. 1).

Again, this definition matches the previous definition of addiction well and helps us to understand what this behavior might look like in an individual client. While the categories continue to be refined, any excessive behavior could cause intrapersonal and interpersonal problems and might lead an individual to seek clinical care. Ultimately, the simplest way of understanding the difference between a behavioral addiction and a healthy enthusiasm is that healthy enthusiasms add to life whereas addictions detract from it (Sun et al., 2012). Continued focus on behavioral addictions will improve our understanding of these concerns and improve clinical effectiveness.

Behavioral Addictions and Substance Abuse Disorders: Are they the same?

As mentioned above, behavioral addictions share much in common with substance abuse disorders. However, care must be taken to compare the addictive behaviors of both substance and behavioral addictions to determine whether these out of control behavioral addictions constitute an addictive process akin to substance related addictions (Ascher et al., 2015). Substance abuse, as compared to the definition for behavioral addictions above, is characterized by the obsession or compulsion to use a substance, particularly where the person lacks control of the use despite knowledge of negative consequences associated with use. Core behaviors shared between the two categories of disorders are listed below:

1. An urge to engage in a behavior with negative consequences
2. Mounting tension unless the behavior is completed
3. Rapid but temporary reduction of the urge after completion of the behavior
4. Return of the urge over hours, days, or weeks
5. External cues unique to the behavior
6. Secondary conditioning by external and internal cues and
7. Hedonic feeling early in the addiction. (Jon E. Grant, 2008)

Behavioral addictions can further be understood in relation to the six following core clinical characteristics:

1. *Salience* – The behavior becomes the most important activity in a person's life
2. *Mood Modification* – The behavior serves as a way to cope or manage negative affect.
3. *Tolerance* – Increasing amounts of the behavior are required to obtain the mood modifying impacts
4. *Withdrawal Symptoms* – There are unpleasant physical or psychological impacts of abstaining from the behavior.
5. *Conflict* – There is considerable negative impact on relationships and responsibilities as a result of the behavior.
6. *Relapse* – There is a strong tendency to repeatedly engage in the behavior. (Rosenberg & Feder, 2014)

These formulations of the clinical components of behavioral addictions bear strong similarities to substance use disorders. Because these features are shared by both substance and impulse control disorders, behavioral addictions, as the term suggests, are considered "addictions without the drugs."

Biological Drive for Pleasure and Relief of Tension

Considering behavioral addictions within the frame of substance abuse allows for the consideration of client pleasure as they engage in these behaviors. Individuals with a gambling addiction might look forward to a trip where they are able to spend time in a casino, and engaging in the pleasurable activity will decrease the anxiety that had built from the increasing cravings they experienced prior to the behavior (Grant 2008). Also, neurobiology research on individuals engaging in impulsive behavior shows that the same neurotransmitters and neuro-circuits are implicated in both substance use disorders and behavioral addictions (more on that later) (Sun et al., 2012). Simply put, the same biological drive for pleasure and relief of tension that may push an individual towards habitual drug use can also drive an individual towards the potential for a monetary reward (pathological gambling), a sexual encounter (in compulsive sexual behaviors) and a food binge (in binge eating disorder).

High Comorbidity

Furthermore, substance use disorders often occur at the same time as a behavioral addictions (Potenza, 2006). The high comorbidity of these disorders suggests comparable mechanisms for their development in an individual client. Both behavioral addictions and substance addictions are also most often initiated during adolescence and young adulthood. Additional evidence for similarities comes from the consequences of these disorders. Financial and martial problems are common, as are feelings of isolation and interpersonal difficulties.

Key Differences Between Substance and Behavioral Addictions

However, there are also some key differences between the two. Firstly, though clients may report feelings of dysphoria when unable to participate in their behavioral addiction that might resemble withdrawal, there are no physical ramifications for stopping the behavior (Sun et al., 2012). Also significant is that while research and brain imaging has shown that behavioral addictions can have similar impacts on neurobiology, the impacts can only ever be indirect, unlike a substance that directly alters brain chemistry. Tolerance is also a key difference. While behavioral addictions may increase in frequency over time, there is no physiological tolerance that builds up for the behavior.

The Brain and Addiction – A Very Abbreviated Discussion of Biology

There are a number of different neurobiological models that help explain what might cause behavioral addictions, each emphasizing a different part of brain functionality. For the purposes of this text we will review the reward cycle (Rosenberg & Feder, 2014). Overall, this can be summarized by the idea that the human brain seeks to drive us to participate in rewarding activities because this helps us survive. Behavioral addictions disturb the natural reward cycle and misdirect activity towards destructive patterns. For a broader discussion of brain chemistry in relation to addictive patterns please see the resources listed at the end of this chapter.

Neuroimaging Studies

Advanced technologies have enabled us only recently to map the human brain and the functions of its various regions more specifically. Scientists now can observe the process of how our brain determines our behavior. This particularly allows us to gain knowledge about behavioral addictions, and is part of the argument for why these disorders should be included in a similar category as substance use disorders (Ascher et al., 2015). Functional neuroimaging studies have shown that gambling, shopping, orgasm, playing video games, and the sight of appetizing food may activate the same parts of the brain as addictive substances (Rosenberg & Feder, 2014).

A Brain Disease

The National Institute on Drug Abuse indicates that addiction is a brain disease resulting from the interactions between salience/reward, learning/ memory/conditioning, and lowered inhibition/control (Abuse, 2014). The reward cycle literature suggests that whenever there is a reward sensed by certain brain regions (the nucleus accumbens and ventral tegmental area) because of a certain substance or behavior, the brain will pay particular attention to those behaviors (Sun et al., 2012). As a result, they will be remembered and reinforced through the amygdala and the hippocampus, which are responsible for conditioning and memory. Continued exposure to the rewarding experiences may weaken a person's inhibitory and control capacity (executed by the prefrontal cortex and regions of anterior cingulate gyrus). These elements combined result in a motivational push to engage in the behavior or use the substance, regardless of the potential consequences.

Prefrontal Cortex Dysfunction

Other categories that the behavioral addictions fall under have slightly different estimates of how brain functioning is involved in the addictive process (Potenza, Koran, Pallanti, 2009). For example, impulsive and compulsive spectrum disorders (hoarding disorder fits on the compulsive scale whereas kleptomania is classified in the impulsive scale, though both may fall under the umbrella of behavioral addictions) may involve inhibitory neurotransmitters such as serotonin and also excitatory neurotransmitters such as glutamate and dopamine along with prefrontal cortex and/or limbic dysfunction. Increased frontal lobe activities may characterize the compulsive disorder class, whereas decreased frontal lobe activity may characterize the impulsive disorders. A more complete discussion of the impulsive and compulsive scale will be discussed next, but both seem to be related to prefrontal cortex dysfunction.

Impulsivity and Compulsivity – A Behavioral Addictions Perspective

The American Psychological Association defines compulsivity as the performance of repetitive behaviors with the goal of reducing or preventing anxiety or distress, not providing pleasure or gratification. Impulsivity refers to an individual's inability to control urges to engage in behaviors that are affecting them in adverse ways. Historically, psychologists have seen impulsivity and compulsivity as diametrically opposed (Grant, 2008). In reality, the relationship is more intricate and behavioral addictions have at times been conceptualized as part of the obsessive-compulsive spectrum (in the DSM-5, as mentioned above, hoarding disorder, trichotillomania, and excoriation are all listed under this category) and the impulsive disorder spectrum. Understanding how obsessive compulsive disorder subtypes such as hoarding share common clinical features with certain behavioral addictions may improve treatment outcomes. For example, assessments can focus on both compulsive shopping and hoarding. Psychotherapeutic interventions might work to target problems with decision making strategies that may be useful in treating both types of disorders, or identifying pharmacological intervention that may target one or the other of them.

Sarah Shops: A Case Study

Sarah, 25, comes into her first session reporting a history of uncontrollable buying that had started in late adolescence. She had become preoccupied with buying things and thought about her shopping trips throughout her entire day. She loves the attention of store staff and notes that it makes her feel like she is important. The thrill that she feels while shopping is replaced with a sense of relief after she leaves the store on her five-times-a-week trips. Sarah typically purchases lotions and other bathroom products, often buying multiples of the same product and keeping them unused in her closet. Sarah lies to her close friends and family about her routines and hides her shopping habits from them by leaving her office early or coming in late to accommodate shopping trips. She has begun to feel increasingly isolated from her social network. Unable to pay for her credit card bills, she has opened multiple accounts to allow herself to continue shopping.

Diagnosing Sarah

Sarah is struggling with compulsive buying, also called compulsive shopping. Given the discussion of substance use disorders above, it is easy to see how this story fits into that clinical picture. You might also make an argument for categorizing it as an impulse control disorder, because she seems unable to control her urges and engages in the behavior excessively. Impulsivity may play an important role in the early stages of her behavioral addiction to shopping and later the behavior becomes more compulsive after a period of habit formation (Potenza et al. 2009).

Final Thoughts

Armed with the definitions of addiction, impulsivity and compulsivity, we can draw some conclusions about behavioral addictions (Ascher et al., 2015; Jon E. Grant, 2008; Rosenberg & Feder, 2014; Sun et al., 2012). First, we can infer that in general behavioral addictions can be conceptualized as similar to impulse control disorders and substance use disorders because they are pleasure seeking. A reward circuit model of addiction helps to conceptualize these disorders from a biological perspective. We can also believe that while comparison to substance use disorder is one way to clinically conceptualize behavioral addictions, not all impulse control disorders fit neatly into this category. In general, behavioral addictions and impulse control disorders are different, both in clinical presentation and intervention, from obsessive compulsive spectrum disorders. But some impulse control disorders may be closer to the family of OCD, or other categories of disorders than to the category of addiction. A layperson, or even inexperienced clinician, may use all of the terms above interchangeably, and ultimately the goal is to treat each individual patient as appropriately as possible within a framework that makes sense for their symptoms. In the upcoming chapter we will discuss different specific behavioral addictions in more detail.

References

Abuse, N. I. o. D. (2014). Drugs, Brains, and Behavior: The Science of Addiction. Retrieved from https://www.drugabuse.gov/publications/drugs-brains-behavior-science-addiction/preface

Alavi, S. S., Ferdosi, M., Jannatifard, F., Eslami, M., Alaghemandan, H., & Setare, M. (2012). Behavioral Addiction versus Substance Addiction: Correspondence of Psychiatric and Psychological Views. *International Journal of Preventive Medicine, 3*(4), 290–294.

American Psychiatric Association. (2000). *Diagnostic and statistical manual of mental disorders* (4th ed., text rev.). doi:10.1176/appi.books.9780890423349.

Ascher, M. S., Levounis, P., & American Psychiatric Association. (2015). *The Behavioral Addictions* (First edition. ed.). Washington, DC: American Psychiatric Publishing, a division of American Psychiatric Association.

Association, A. P. (2013a). Highlights of Changes From DSM-IV-TR to DSM-5. Retrieved from http://www.dsm5.org/Documents/changes from dsm-iv-tr to dsm-5.pdf

Association, A. P. (2013b, 5/16/2013). Substance Related and Addictive Disorders. Retrieved from http://www.dsm5.org/documents/substance use disorder fact sheet.pdf

Grant, J. E. (2008). *Impulse control disorders: a clinician's guide to understanding and treating behavioral addictions* (1st ed.). New York: W.W. Norton.

Medicine, A. S. f. A. (2011). Definition of Addiction.

Potenza, M. N. (2009). Non-substance and substance addictions. *Addiction (Abingdon, England), 104*(6), 1016–1017. http://doi.org/10.1111/j.1360-0443.2009.02619.x

Potenza, M. N., Koran, L. M., & Pallanti, S. (2009). The relationship between impulse control disorders and obsessive-compulsive disorder: a current understanding and future research directions. *Psychiatry Research, 170*(1), 22–31. http://doi.org/10.1016/j.psychres.2008.06.036

Rosenberg, K. P., & Feder, L. C. (2014). *Behavioral addictions: criteria, evidence, and treatment.* London ; Waltham, MA: Academic Press.

Sun, A.-P., Ashley, L. L., & Dickson, L. (2012). *Behavioral Addiction: Screening, Assessment, and Treatment.* Las Vegas, NV: Central Recovery Press.

Chapter 1 Resources

This section gives a list of resources for those who wish to seek out more information on the topics presented in the chapter. When considering the history and changes to the DSM surrounding behavioral addictions, please note that many resources were created prior to the release of the DSM-5 in 2013, as such many references may include diagnostic information from an earlier edition of the DSM.

Printed Resources

The following books/chapters are selections that may help deepen your knowledge of subjects in this chapter.

The Behavioral Addictions, Ascher and Levounis
Chapter 1: Helping People Behave Themselves: Identifying and Treating Behavioral Addictions

Behavioral Addictions: Criteria, Evidence, and Treatment, Rosenberg and Feder
Chapter 1: An Introduction to Behavioral Addictions
Chapter 2: Behavioral Addiction: The Nexus of Impulsivity and Compulsivity

Behavioral Addictions: Screening, Assessment and Treatment, An-Pyng Sun, PhD
Chapter 1: Historical Background of Behavioral Addiction and the Trend Today

Impulse Control Disorders, Grant
Chapter 1: Clinical Characteristics of Impulse Control Disorders
Chapter 2: Models for Understanding Impulse Control Disorders
Chapter 3: The Compulsive-Impulsive Spectrum: The Compulsive Aspects of Impulse Control Disorders
Chapter 4: The Relationship of Impulse Control Disorders to Drug and Alcohol Addiction

Online Resources

The American Psychiatric Association has an extremely useful website on the DSM-5. From the main page you can access presentations on research used to inform changes as well as documents highlighting the changes for many major disorders.
http://www.dsm5.org/Pages/Default.aspx

The American Addictions Center also has a useful website with information about behavioral addictions: http://americanaddictioncenters.org/behavioral-addictions/

Behavioral Addictions vs. Substance Addictions
https://www.psychologytoday.com/blog/addicted-brains/201306/behavioral-addictions-vs-substance-addictions

Journal Articles

Alavi, S. S., Ferdosi, M., Jannatifard, F., Eslami, M., Alaghemandan, H., & Setare, M. (2012). Behavioral Addiction versus Substance Addiction: Correspondence of Psychiatric and Psychological Views. *International Journal of Preventive Medicine, 3*(4), 290–294.
http://www.ncbi.nlm.nih.gov/pmc/articles/PMC3354400/

Brevers, D., & Noel, X. (n.d.). Commentary on: Are we overpathologizing everyday life? A tenable blueprint for behavioral addiction research: On functional and compulsive aspects of reinforcement pathologies. *Journal of Behavioral Addictions, 4*(3), 135–138. http://doi.org/10.1556/2006.4.2015.017

Billieux, J., Schimmenti, A., Khazaal, Y., Maurage, P., & Heeren, A. (n.d.). Are we overpathologizing everyday life? A tenable blueprint for behavioral addiction research. *Journal of Behavioral Addictions, 4*(3), 119–123. http://doi.org/10.1556/2006.4.2015.009

Brewer JA, Potenza MN. The neurobiology and genetics of impulse control disorders: relationships to drug addictions. *Biochem Pharmacol.* 2008;*75(1)*:63–75.

Grant, J. E., Potenza, M. N., Weinstein, A., & Gorelick, D. A. (2010). Introduction to Behavioral Addictions. *The American Journal of Drug and Alcohol Abuse, 36*(5), 233–241. http://doi.org/10.3109/00952990.2010.491884

Potenza, M. N. (2009). Non-substance and substance addictions. *Addiction (Abingdon, England), 104*(6), 1016–1017. http://doi.org/10.1111/j.1360-0443.2009.02619.x
https://www.ncbi.nlm.nih.gov/pmc/articles/PMC2865686/

Potenza, M. N., Koran, L. M., & Pallanti, S. (2009). The relationship between impulse control disorders and obsessive-compulsive disorder: a current understanding and future research directions. *Psychiatry Research, 170*(1), 22–31. http://doi.org/10.1016/j.psychres.2008.06.036

Yau, Y. H. C., & Potenza, M. N. (2015). Gambling Disorder and Other Behavioral Addictions: Recognition and Treatment. *Harvard Review of Psychiatry*, *23*(2), 134–146. http://doi.org/10.1097/HRP.0000000000000051

Internet Videos

An Overview of Behavioral Addictions
https://www.youtube.com/watch?v=PaU5geYu98U

Everything you know about addiction is wrong
https://www.youtube.com/watch?v=PY9DcIMGxMs

Behavioral Addictions for Beginners
https://www.youtube.com/watch?v=_wZk8QxrKDY

Dr. Patrick Carnes – Chemical Addictions vrs. Process/Behavioral Addictions
https://www.youtube.com/watch?v=0mbbcPO8_h8

What role do genetics play in behavioral addictions?
https://www.youtube.com/watch?v=5tpLbNK7n50

Technology Addiction and other Behavioral Addictions
https://www.youtube.com/watch?v=5ycoPFTHnjA

Process Addictions – Part I
https://www.youtube.com/watch?v=djnLz3J2YF0

National Organizations

National Institute on Drug Abuse (NIDA), https://www.drugabuse.gov/
National Institute on Alcohol Abuse and Alcoholism (NIAAA), https://www.niaaa.nih.gov/
National Institute of Mental Health (NIMH), https://www.nimh.nih.gov/index.shtml
Center for Substance Abuse Treatment (CSAT), http://www.samhsa.gov/about-us/who-we-are/offices-centers/csat
Substance Abuse and Mental Health Services Administration (SAMHSA), http://www.samhsa.gov/
Anxiety and Depression Association of America (ADAA), https://www.adaa.org/

CHAPTER 2

Types of Behavioral Addictions

Chapter Overview

The purpose of this chapter is to provide an overview of the various types of behavioral addictions. We've mentioned many of them in passing and now we will focus on providing definitions and a brief understanding of each type of addiction. This chapter will also aim to identify key similarities and differences between the disorders and address the concept of clients with multiple behavioral addictions as well as comorbidity with other mental health issues.

In this chapter each behavioral addiction or group of addictions gets its own mini-chapter with the following sub-sections: 1. History and Epidemiology, 2. Clinical Presentation and Diagnostic Options, 3. Comorbidity. Where appropriate, some behavioral addictions are described in combined categories. The brevity of this coverage is designed to increase its utility and allow it serve as a convenient reference guide. Please refer to the extensive additional resources section at the end of this book for more information on individual behavioral additions. In the next chapter you will find case studies for many of the categories of behavioral addiction considered here. These are designed to illustrate each of the disorders and enable you to see the ways in which they effect people and their impact their lives.

Comorbidity and Addiction

Comorbidity is when two or more disorders or illnesses occur in the same person (NIDA, 2012). These issues can occur at the same time or in succession and comorbidity implies that there are interactions between the disorders or illness that can impact the severity of both. Addictions are commonly co-occurring with other mental health concerns, a fact that has been documented in national surveys since the 1980s (NIDA, 2012). For example, with substance abuse, data shows that an individual diagnosed with a mood or anxiety disorder is twice as likely to suffer from a substance use disorder. The trend is likely similar for behavioral addictions. In this chapter we will consider some of the commonly co-occurring concerns with each behavioral addiction. Continued research into effective treatments for behavioral addictions will help assist clinicians treating individual patients, as clients often have a complicated mixture of issues presenting at the same time, and one issue may impact treatment efficacy of the other.

How Co-Occurring Addictions Can Impact Each Other

Co-occurring addictions specifically impact each other in ways that are important for a clinician to understand (Sun et al., 2012). Some additive behaviors will increase together, such as drinking and gambling. Other addictions will alternate in severity, one addiction mediating the withdrawal impacts of another. Sometimes, an addict with complete treatment in one addiction only to engage in a new one. Additionally, addicts will at times use a less shameful form of addiction to mask another. To summarize how one addiction might influence another, the following five categories may be helpful:

1. *Intensifying* – when addictive behaviors take place at the same time and encourage one another.
2. *Ritualizing* – when one addiction behavior precedes another in a habitual/ritual process.
3. *Numbing* – when one addictive behavior allows for another to occur by reducing distress or anxiety
4. *Combining* – where addictive behaviors are combined for a particularly potent "high"
5. *Cycling* – when an addict completes treatment for one addiction and replaces it with a new, similarly functioning addiction (in part from (Sun et al., 2012)

Comorbid addictions complicate the diagnostic and treatment picture and suggest that treatments that do not address underlying concerns will not be effective in the long term. Careful consideration of the relationship between co-occurring concerns is essential for effective treatment.

Gambling Addiction

History and Epidemiology

Gambling addiction is one of the most thoroughly studied behavioral addictions and gambling-related issues have been documented for nearly as long as gambling has existed. Gambling as a form of recreation has been a popular human activity for millennia. In ancient Greece, where organized gaming was part of daily life, an overzealous Emperor Commodus may have directly contributed to the fall of the Roman Empire with his irresponsible gambling habits (Rosenberg & Feder, 2014). Dice have been found in ancient Egyptian tombs and a gaming board is cut into the steps of the Acropolis (Sun et al., 2012). Though gambling addiction has been observed for some time, it was not included in the DSM formally until the third edition in 1980. As discussed in Chapter one, pathological gambling was changed in the revised DSM-5 to part of the category of "Substance Use and Addictive Disorders" representing a shift in the understanding of the etiology and clinical presentation of this disorder. Additionally, consistently high rates of comorbidity with substance use also supports its inclusion in this category.

In the United States, gambling is a large, lucrative industry, reporting annual revenues of over $34 billion (Rosenberg & Feder, 2014). The vast majority of individuals who gamble do so for fun and do not suffer any adverse impacts due to their participation. Nearly 85% of all Americans reported having gambled at least once in their lives (Sun et al., 2012). An estimated 0.4-5.3% of people worldwide, however, suffer enormous consequences when gambling becomes a diagnosable behavioral addiction, or even the sub-clinical concern, problematic gambling. The large range of prevalence rates are likely due to differences in survey methodology. Current estimates of prevalence in the United States range from 5-6%: that is to say 5-6% of the adult gambling population experiences significant problems as a result of gambling (Sun et al., 2012).

Clinical Presentation and Diagnostic Options

Excessive gambling has the potential to disrupt an individual's functioning in all spheres of their life and is associated with physical and psychological distress, financial and legal difficulties, academic and/or employment disruptions, and family and relationship discord. To complicate matters for clinicians, gambling addiction is sometimes referred to as the "hidden addiction" as it cannot be detected physically – there are no medical tests for it (Sun et al., 2012). As a result, it can be much easier for a client to hide their level of involvement, and their addiction may progress more quickly. The DSM-5 presents the following diagnostic criteria for pathological gambling disorder:

1. Needs to gamble with increasing amounts of money in order to achieve the desired excitement.
2. Is restless or irritable when attempting to cut down or stop gambling.
3. Has made repeated unsuccessful efforts to control, cut back, or stop gambling.
4. Is often preoccupied with gambling (e.g., having persistent thoughts of reliving past gambling experiences, handicapping or planning the next venture, thinking of ways to get money with which to gamble).
5. Often gambles when feeling distressed (e.g., helpless, guilty, anxious, depressed).
6. After losing money gambling, often returns another day to get even ("chasing" one's losses).
7. Lies to conceal the extent of involvement with gambling.
8. Has jeopardized or lost a significant relationship, job, or educational or career opportunity because of gambling.
9. Relies on others to provide money to relieve desperate financial situations caused by gambling (APA 2013).

Of the above criteria, four (or more) of the nine listed are required for a diagnosis.

Certain individuals may be more at risk for gambling addictions. Research results show that there may be a neurobiological and genetic risk factor for developing pathological gambling; impacted individuals may be pre-disposed to deficits in dopamine which puts them at high risk for pleasure-generating addictions (Sun et al., 2012). Another risk factor is history of trauma: a recent study showed that 64% of the individuals in treatment for gambling addiction in one study had history of abuse (Sun et al., 2012). Additional risk factors include age, male gender, social modeling, personality risk factors including impulsivity and sensation seeking traits, poorly developed coping skills, low self-esteem, and lack of social support. As with all addictions, no specific trait can be identified and the traits or client history listed above should be considered risk factors, not as causal factors. In other words, they are associated with behavioral addictions and may enable or increase the chances of having them, but they are not necessarily responsible for producing them.

Comorbidity

There is a very high incidence of comorbid disorders and pathological gambling. Some of these co-occurring disorders may be behavioral addictions themselves, including compulsive shopping and compulsive sexual behavior, which highlights the impulsive and dysfunctional nature of these excessive behaviors (Sun et al., 2012). Suicide and substance abuse are also highly linked with gambling disorders. Research has shown that individuals using alcohol and other drugs are six times more likely than the general population to develop a gambling problem. A recent study suggested that substance use disorder preceded gambling disorder for the majority of pathological gamblers with both diagnoses. In addition to the already-mentioned issues, pathological gambling is highly comorbid with affective disorders such as major depressive disorder and bipolar disorder and with ADHD. Though there has been some research on causality, individual patients will likely have unique profiles of correlated issues that all may interact and therefore perpetuate one another. A highly trained clinician will help to focus attention to highest priority issues and in some cases, work to address underlying concerns.

Sexual Addictions

History and Epidemiology

Sexual addictions are historically one of the most misunderstood, mislabeled and stigmatized category of addictions. Media portrayals of sex addicts suggest that they participate in treatment only for exposure to other individuals who they can engage with sexually, or at other times, simply vilify sex addicts as individuals with poor character. Social taboos around sexual behavior are some of the most salient. The DSM does not recognize a specific disorder for sexual addiction (Ascher et al., 2015). In 1987, a revised version of the DSM-III referred to a pattern of "repeated sexual conquests or other forms of non-paraphilic sexual addiction" but this was later removed and the DSM-IV and DSM-5 did not directly include sexual addictions, though a

Sexual Disorders NOS remained in the DSM-IV (APA, 1987, 2013). Though sexual addictions were considered for inclusion in the recently published DSM-5, the APA ultimately decided that there is not enough peer-reviewed evidence to establish the diagnostic criteria and support inclusion of this behavior as an independent disorder (APA 2013).

Currently the prevalence of sexual addiction is estimated to be somewhere between 3% and 6% of the general population, though prevalence changes depending on certain characteristics such as age and gender (Rosenberg & Feder, 2014). Though the DSM-5 did not include a formal diagnosis for sexual addiction, the call for more research and continued clinical focus is clear within the literature.

Clinical Presentation and Diagnostic Options

Sexual addiction is described as an intimacy disorder manifested as a compulsive cycle of preoccupation, ritualization, sexual behavior or sexual anorexia (excessive control over sexual behavior), and despair (Sun et al., 2012). Sex addicts have a lack of control over their behavior, serious consequences both personally and professionally, and use sexual behaviors as a primary coping strategy. Sex addiction is often considered distinct from pedophilia as it does not have an abnormal object of sexual desire, but rather involves the excessive practice of otherwise normal sexual behavior. However, some of the behaviors commonly associated with sex addiction (prostitution, compulsive viewing of Internet pornography, among others) may be less "normal". Sexual acts for an individual with a sex addiction are often used to escape and soothe negative feelings. Though there are differences among various approaches to sexual addiction these core features overlap and may be useful to help a clinician distinguish between normal and abnormal sexual behavior:

1. Excessive sexual behavior, generally outside the context of sustained relationships
2. Intense and persistent urges to perform such sexual behavior, similar to the drug craving found in chemical addictions
3. Continuation of sexual behavior despite the potential to cause significant harm with regard to personal, occupational and financial domains and/or physical health
4. Difficulty stopping the behavior despite repeated attempts or in the face of significant negative consequences (Ascher et al., 2015)

In addition to these elements, tolerance and withdrawal have also been discussed extensively in relation to sexual addictions in the context of debating the utility of using substance addiction models for treatment of sexual addictions. Though patients may experience psychological distress if unable to engage in their sexual addiction behaviors, there is no physical "withdrawal" in the same sense as a chemical addiction. Furthermore, the diagnostic picture is complicated by client awareness and understanding of the behavior. This excessive engagement in otherwise normal behaviors in this addiction, as with other behavioral addictions, can make clinical intervention difficult as clients may see their behavior as enthusiasm for sexual behavior or personal and/or cultural differences.

However, sex addiction has consequences not associated with normative sexual behavior. First, as sexual addictions are often highly secretive and pre-occupying, addicts may suffer socially as they distance themselves from their network of family and friends. The fear of being discovered may cause immense shame and anxiety, and addicts often struggle with the tension between their actions and their personal values and belief systems. As noted earlier, sexual taboos are highly salient elements of culture, and may increase the difficulty of discussing these concerns (Carnes, 2001)

Much like gambling addictions, certain individuals may be more at risk to develop a sexual addition. Because sex serves a biological purpose and releases the neurochemical oxytocin, it has been suggested that oxytocin levels in sex addicts may be deficient/abundance and be partially responsible for the dysfunctional behavior (Sun et al., 2012). Other clinicians believe that sexual dysfunction stems largely from attachment disorders, where individuals have difficulty forming stable bonds with others. Similarly, clients who have history of trauma can potentially manifest their traumatic past in a sexual addiction. Also, cognitive distortions play an important role in sexual addictions. Feelings of worthlessness, negative self-image, fear and distrust of others, among other distorted ways of thinking can lead individuals to the belief that sex will relieve their issues. This creates a cycle as guilt and negative feelings about self are a result of engaging in addiction related behaviors: client is distressed, seeks pleasure and soothing in the form of orgasm, shame and distress at sexual behavior, and the cycle continues.

Comorbidity

Similar to gambling disorders, research around sexual addictions shows a high rates of comorbidity. Because sexuality is intricately tied up with self-esteem and body image, sexual disorders have high comorbidity with eating disorders. Research has estimated that this could be as high as 38% (Carnes, 2001). Substance use is also commonly paired with sexual addictions. About 42% of sex addicts have co-occurring issues with substance use. Among cocaine abusers, estimates show that 50-70% also have issues with sexual compulsions. Additionally, affective disorders are common among sex addicts, and 72% report suicidal ideation. Other compulsive behaviors, such as gambling, shoplifting, compulsive shopping and other forms of behavioral addictions are also common. One study found that of a pool of sex addicts only around 10% reported just one addiction. Trauma also has significantly high rates of comorbidity with sexual addictions. Some research has shown that 97% of sex addicts were emotionally abused as children, 72% were physically abused, and as many as 81% were sexually abused (Sun et al., 2012).

Technology-Related Addictions

History and Epidemiology

Since its creation, the Internet has become an increasingly pervasive part of the daily lives of individuals. We read books, socialize, learn, play and relax as part of an online world. In particular, recent findings around the preoccupying nature of online gaming and social media addiction are gaining traction. Research shows that individuals engaged in online gaming are triggered through similar pathways as a substance abuser (Rosenberg & Feder, 2014). Gaming provides a feeling of pleasure and reward which then encourages repeat use. This pattern of reward may be similar in online gambling, the "in-person" version of which is included in the DSM-5 chapter on Substance Use and Addictive Disorders (APA, 2013). Online gamers play compulsively to the exclusion of other interests, and this activity has significant consequences for their other responsibilities. Internet Gaming Disorder was included under "Conditions for further study" in Section III of the DSM-5 (Association, 2013a). The APA did not feel that there was enough literature to support its inclusion as a disorder, and most of the literature on Internet gaming disorder comes from Asian countries where cultural norms around Internet use may be different than in the United States. Hopefully, the addition in Section III will encourage more research on these developing clinical concerns.

Additionally, at this time, the diagnostic criteria for this condition are limited to Internet gaming and do not include general use of the Internet or social media (APA, 2013). Other potential forms of Internet addictions include cell phone addictions, online shopping addictions, online pornography addictions, or just problematic and intrusive Internet use (Rosenberg & Feder, 2014). Many of these concerns are "online" versions of other behavioral addictions. Some researchers reject the idea that these are Internet addictions and instead suggest that the Internet provides a unique place for them to engage in other addictions. However, others argue that the Internet provides a unique and often private access point, where compulsive and impulsive behaviors are enabled or even rewarded. For example, someone with a compulsive shopping addiction may find online shopping more addictive still because their web-browser saves their credit card automatically, and they may be able to make purchases with only a few clicks, where previously driving to the store was a multi-step process. Or with a different client who is struggling with anxiety over schoolwork, Netflix might provide a welcome and addicting distraction to the work she needs to complete. Thus, though there are similarities to "offline" behavioral addictions, the unique elements of online addictions require specific awareness and clinical intervention, justifying their consideration separately.

Clinical Presentation and Diagnostic Options

Like the other behavioral addictions discussed in this book, Internet addictions are characterized by the habitual compulsion to engage in a certain activity, regardless of the associated consequences (Rosenberg & Feder, 2014). Rather than dealing with stressors constructively, the Internet is used for self-soothing, and when access is limited there may be psychological symptoms of withdrawal. As noted above, there are a number of versions of Internet addictions which all present different clinical symptoms, though these core elements are similar. Internet additions (sometimes referred to as technological addictions) are sometimes placed into five sub-categories: 1. cybersexual addiction, 2. cyber-relationship addiction, 3. net compulsions, 4. information overload, and 5. computer addiction (Kimberly S. Young, 2011). This conceptualization however, lacks inclusion of addictions such as Internet gambling, where Internet is the medium in which an addict engages in the behavior. Others suggest the following list of categories of Internet addiction: 1. online gaming addiction, 2. information overload, 3. online gambling, 4. online shopping, 5. cyber-sexual addiction, 6. cyber-relationship addiction (Sun et al., 2012). Ultimately, both categorizations suggest that the Internet is a platform exceptionally well suited to the engagement in problematic behaviors.

Regardless of the form that Internet addiction takes, diagnosis can be complex (Young, 2011). The Internet for many people is an essential part of daily life and an incredible tool that has advanced our society. In many ways, the Internet is a benefit to individual clients, who can even access apps for relaxation and anxiety reduction. Identifying when use has surpassed a clinically significant level can be extremely challenging. Furthermore, questions about Internet use may not even be included in typical intake interview as the disorder currently has very little recognition in the broad field of mental health. Diagnosis should focus on how Internet use no longer is something the client can easily control, as well as understanding the individual consequences of continued use, and working with clients to understand underlying issues that may be causing them to seek relief.

Currently, few clear criteria are available for diagnosing Internet addictions that are not recognized as a specific disorder in the most recent DSM-5. As parallels between pathological gambling and Internet addition exist, some of the diagnostic criteria in pathological gambling can be modified to apply to Internet addictions. Some of the following criteria might be helpful for consideration:

- Internet addicts, as compared to other users, demonstrate a loss of impulse control: despite consequences, addicts continue use
- Average online usage is excessive and basic tasks are interrupted (for example: sleep deprivation, and then resulting patterns of lateness to work or school, or basic hygiene needs are skipped)
- Client has made sever unsuccessful efforts to control, cut back or stop their use
- The Internet serves as a way to regulate mood
- The client stays online longer than intended and may lie to others about the extent of their use. (Kimberly S. Young, 2011)

In addition, a client may exhibit signs of distress when use is reduced. Preoccupation with Internet usage may serve as important criteria for understanding an individual client's potential Internet addiction. In 2004 Widyanto and McMurren created the Internet Addiction Test, the first validated instrument to assess Internet addiction. This test may help provide an assessment of specific issues created by a client's Internet usage and a starting point for discussion (Kimberly S. Young, 2011).

Early research on the prevalence of Internet addictions estimate that nearly 6% of Internet users fit the profile for Internet addiction, though prevalence statistics vary widely across cultures (Kimberly S. Young, 2011). Another recent study showed that one in eight Americans shows at least one of the signs of Internet addiction. Higher rates of prevalence have been found among college age populations, potentially explained by their level of access to the Internet and encouraged use. Adolescents are also a vulnerable group for development of an Internet addiction. International studies, which make up the bulk of research on this issue, show even higher prevalence rates. One study done in India said that almost 40% of Internet users show signs of heavy usage, with the bulk of that group from young, college-going males. Overall, there are some difficulties in comparing prevalence rates directly as differences in study methodologies may dramatically impact the results. However, though more research must be done on prevalence, most studies show consistently that college students may be at the highest risk for developing a variety of Internet addictions. Armed with this knowledge, clinicians can include relevant questions about Internet addictions when they are treating high risk individuals, especially those with other comorbid concerns.

Outside of the neurochemical cycles associated with our basic understanding of addiction, where the brain's reward network is involved in habit forming around addictive behaviors, individuals with Internet addictions tend to have additional mental health issues that may contribute significantly to their struggles (Kimberly S. Young, 2011; Rosenberg & Feder, 2014). For example, some Internet addiction researchers suggest that young people are using the Internet as compensation for self-identity, self-expression and social networking (Kimberly S. Young, 2011). Internet addicts, in general, struggle to form intimate relationships and may use the anonymity of the online world to mask their own insecurities and connect with others in a non-threatening environment (Kimberly S. Young, 2011). Clinicians need to be aware than individuals who struggle to form stable social support networks might be vulnerable to Internet addictions, and also should consider the client's social needs when developing a treatment plan to address addiction.

Comorbidity

Often, Internet addicts suffer from multiple addictions. Clients with history of drug or alcohol abuse might identify the Internet as a safer way to fulfill their addictive tendencies and simply switch focus without addressing the underlying concerns (Kimberly S. Young, 2011). Other studies have shown that substance use and problematic Internet use are linked (Rosenberg & Feder, 2014). Multiple addictions mean greater potential for relapse and Internet addictions are especially tough as usage for work or school can increase temptation to return to problematic usage. Other disorders can also impact treatment outcomes. Specifically, depression and other affective disorders (AHDH and generalized anxiety disorder) are linked with Internet addiction (Rosenberg & Feder, 2014). Though a causal relationship has yet to be explored fully in the research, some research has found that depression is the most influential risk factor for Internet addiction (Sun et al., 2012).

Outside of addiction comorbidity, Internet addictions are often comorbid with underlying interpersonal difficulty, such as introversion and social awkwardness (Kimberly S. Young, 2011). Many Internet addicts are unable to communicate effectively in face-to-face interactions and communicating online may seem safer and easier. Others have limited social support and turn to online communities for connection. A study done in 2003 found that 63% of attorneys polled said online affairs were the leading cause of divorce. And whether an affair is going on or not, preoccupation with the Internet and an online world can lead to disconnection in primary relationships, ironically often the opposite of what addicts sought out to soothe.

Ultimately, whether Internet addiction stems from a previous addiction or psychiatric concern or causes them, it is important to screen and treat these concerns alongside Internet addiction in order to improve treatment outcomes and long term effectiveness.

Food Related Addictions

History and Epidemiology

Eating disorders are among some of the most common yet serious psychological problems in the United States (Sun et al., 2012). Even for individuals without disordered eating habits food is often described as addicting, and you might hear someone talk about his or her strained "relationship" with food. Advertising for certain foods reflects public attitudes about how avoiding sugar and fat can be impossible: "once you pop you can't stop" for example (Ascher et al., 2015). In studies done with laboratory rats, when the rats were provided with access to a sugar/fat solution for two hours, they consumed more than their typical daily energy intake, thus demonstrating a lack of control when exposed to these highly palatable foods (Ascher et al., 2015). After a period of abstinence from sugar the rats will consume more sugar when re-exposed and in the interim even show physical symptoms of withdrawal. Though humans are not rats, our response to highly palatable foods is very similar. Furthermore, with increasingly engineered and chemically enhanced food entering the human diet, understanding eating trends will be extremely important.

Research about the impact of high sugar and high fat diets, demonstrates that similar neural pathways to substance addiction are at work with food addictions. Additionally, unlike other behavioral addictions, food addictions have a direct chemical impact on the brain rather than simply a psychological impact. Again, there is controversy and clinical complexity that stems from the fact that eating is a necessary part of healthy life. Determining the point where eating patterns exceed personal preference and transition into addictive behavior can be a gray area. However, similarities including loss of control, tolerance and withdrawal, and neurochemical processes involved in highly rewarding food make considering binge eating disorder and other behavioral food addictions within the category of substance use a useful tool for clinicians. Conceptualizing food addictions in similar terms to substance use disorders will help clinicians assist the millions of individuals who struggle with food-related concerns with interventions tailored to treat the addiction cycle.

Generally speaking, eating pathologies are characterized by maladaptive attitudes and behaviors relating to eating, weight, and body image. The DSM-5 created a new chapter called "Feeding and Eating Disorders" to group together clinically related concerns under one chapter and credentialed a new disorder, Binge Eating Disorder. Overeating also has significant public health implications. In the United states, obesity rates for adults reached 36.5% in 2015 (CDC, 2016). Though often labeled a developed world issue and associated with certain stereotypes of the US, outside of the United States, an estimated 115 million people suffer from obesity related issues. Rates of obesity are significant because of the associated health concerns: in 2008, costs of obesity related medical concerns in the United States totaled over $147 billion. This number has continued to increase, and obesity remains the second- leading cause of preventable death in the US.

While obesity continues to rise, significant efforts have been poured into providing tools to help individuals reduce body weight and maintain healthier habits (Rosenberg & Feder, 2014). These statistics help to illuminate the considerable issues created by food related mental health concerns. While obesity and binge eating disorder are not necessarily interchangeable terms, the point remains clear – further investigation into food related addictions could have wide reaching implications for a serious global health concern.

Clinical Presentation and Diagnostic Options

As discussed above, the DSM-5 includes a newly added category of Binge Eating Disorder as a review of the previously used Eating Disorders NOS (Not Otherwise Specified) category found that most often this non-specific category was being used to diagnose individuals who were bingeing in the absence of any compensatory activity, such as purging. The following diagnostic criteria were established to define binge eating disorder:

1. Eating in a short period of time an amount of food that is definitely larger than most people would eat in a similar period of time under similar circumstances
2. a sense of lack of control over eating during the episode (for example, a feeling that one cannot stop eating or control what or how much one is eating)
3. Recurrent episodes of binge eating, characterized by a sense of lack of control over eating during the episode.
4. The binge-eating episodes are associated with three (or more) of the following:

   o eating much more rapidly than normal
   o eating until feeling uncomfortably full
   o eating large amounts of food when not feeling physically hungry
   o eating alone because of feeling embarrassed by how much one is eating
   o feeling disgusted with oneself, depressed, or very guilty afterwards

5. Marked distress regarding binge eating is present.
6. The binge eating occurs, on average, at least once a week for three months.

In addition to the listed criteria, these binging episodes must be unconnected to purging or periods of restriction that would categorize the behavior in a different Feeding and Eating Disorder Category. Another helpful way of conceptualizing a patient's food concerns as a food addiction comes from the Yale Food Addiction Scale:

Does your patient:

Have control over his or her eating?
Eat more than he or she intended?
Drink excessive soda and sugary drinks?
Feel addicted to fast food?
Think about eating fatty or sugary foods multiple times a day?
Try and fail to cut down on his or her eating?
Gain weight despite attempts to cut down?
Gain weight despite numerous health and life consequences?

Additional items from the YFAS may also be useful for clinicians working with food addicted clients.

There are a number of factors that may increase an individual's risk for developing a food addiction. Many of the individuals who suffer from food addictions and eating disorders use food to alleviate negative emotions that cause them distress (Sun et al., 2012). Individuals may use food as a response to emotional stress, loneliness or other interpersonal conflicts. Thus, those with poor coping mechanisms may be at higher risk for developing addictions. Other personality characteristics may also come into play including low self-esteem and high impulsivity. Family history also suggests that an individual may be at increased risk if there are other close relatives with the same concerns. Certain diets may also be of higher risk. Though almost all food is rewarding to consume – especially if you're very hungry – certain highly palatable foods poses increased addictive qualities due to the importance of these food groups in early human survival (Rosenberg & Feder, 2014). Therefore, individuals with poor nutrition, and high sugar and fat diets may be at higher risk of developing a food addiction.

Comorbidity

As with many behavioral addictions, research shows that food addictions and substance use disorders occur together in rates higher than compared to the general population (Sun et al., 2012). Nearly 50% of female patients with an eating disorder abuse substances, though this prevalence depends on the specific eating disorder in question (for example, anorexia is associated with lower rates of substance abuse whereas binge eating disorder is associated with higher rates of substance abuse). This relationship is clinically significant, and one disorder may stem from another. For example, the weight loss effects of some substances may have a primary reinforcing role in their continued use in patients with a comorbid eating disorder. Outside of co-occurring substance use concerns, patients with food addictions or eating disorders may present with other psychiatric and personality concerns. Attention to interactions between comorbid concerns will be essential for effective treatment.

Impulse Control Disorders

History and Epidemiology

Impulse control disorders are a group of mental health concerns characterized by a repeated inability to resist the urge to engage in a behavior. This category includes kleptomania, pyromania and intermittent explosive disorder. Previously, Impulse Control disorders was a catch all category for many of the behavioral addictions; with the revised DSM-5 many have been moved into more specific chapters, and most notably pathological gambling was moved into the same category as Substance Use and Addictive disorders (APA, 2013). Kleptomania, Pyromania and Intermittent Explosive Disorder remain grouped together in the new chapter on Disruptive, Impulse-Control, and Conduct Disorders. Intermittent Explosive Disorder received changes to the diagnostic criteria and age of potential diagnosis. Controversy continues over whether impulse control disorders are similar enough to addictive disorders to be classified together and also if these concerns share the same underlying pathologies and for that reason might merit parallel treatments (Sun et al., 2012). There is also debate over whether they should be considered formal disorders at all as the prevalence rates are estimated to be very low. In this section we will discuss both Kleptomania and Pyromania at length, and mention other disorders that have been included in this category (though more resources are included at the back of this chapter). These disorders are rarely diagnosed and as such are assumed to be rare, though others argue that other diagnoses better address the behaviors. As a result, there is little research on etiology, prevalence, and treatment options (Sun et al., 2012).

Kleptomania has been recognized since the late 1800s, though people have been stealing for as long as others have been selling (Sun et al., 2012). It was formalized as a diagnosis as it became increasingly clear that in some cases of shoplifting, patients were unable to resist the temptation to steal and the act may be considered involuntary (Rosenberg & Feder, 2014). Kleptomania likely accounts for about 5% of the shoplifting cases in the United States and translates to about 100,000 arrests and a cost of about $500 million dollars annually. Though there has been surprisingly little attention given to kleptomania in scientific literature, prevalence rates are estimated to be between 0.5-1.0% of the general population; when considering clinical population samples, however, such as psychiatric inpatients, the prevalence rates increase dramatically, with some studies showing as much as 9.3% prevalence for lifetime history of kleptomania.

Pyromania, characterized by multiple episodes of fire setting and a powerful attraction to fires, is a rarely diagnosed disorder with a prevalence of about 1% in the general population (Sun et al., 2012). Much like kleptomania, prevalence rates for psychiatric inpatients increase, rising to a lifetime prevalence rate of 6.9%. This disorder is rarely diagnosed: often fire setting can be more accurately explained by the criteria for antisocial personality, conduct disorder or substance intoxication, all of which are exclusionary criteria for pyromania. Pyromania was discussed in the late 1800s as part of Freud's belief that fire was a symbol of sexuality. Other's believed that fire might be a symbol of power and prestige. Pyromania is currently considerably more prevalent in males, particularly those with poor social skills and other learning disabilities, but a cause for this disparity remains unclear.

Intermittent Explosive Disorder (IED) is characterized by recurring outbursts of aggression, often leading to assault on people or property, that are disproportionate to the stressor and not better explained by another diagnosis (Association, 2013a). Immediately following the outburst, the individual may feel a sense of relief, though later they will likely feel regretful (Sun et al., 2012). Though outbursts are typically short lived, their frequency and intensity can lead to legal, relationship and occupational difficulties. Research suggests that IED may be common, with 6.3% of the general population meeting criteria for lifetime IED. Though historically prevalence studies have shown that this disorder is much more common in men, more recent studies suggest the ratio is closer to 1:1 (Sun et al., 2012). Like pyromania, a diagnosis of IED requires ruling out a number of other diagnoses as aggression is a feature of many psychological concerns.

Clinical Presentation and Diagnostic Options

Kleptomania, pyromania, and intermittent explosive disorder (IED) are part of a category of disorders that are characterized by a patients continued engagement in a behavior despite negative consequences, a mounting tension until the behavior is completed, and rapid but temporary resolution of the tension and urges after the behavior is completed (Sun et al., 2012). Assessment and diagnosis are key as many impulse control disorders go undiagnosed (Jon E. Grant, 2008). For many patients, shame and secrecy are key elements of an impulse control disorder, and kleptomania, pyromania and IED may involve illegal or immoral behaviors. Patients with kleptomania and pyromania may believe clinicians are legally bound to report their illegal behaviors. Other patients may simply be unaware that the behaviors they are struggling with may be something a therapist can help them manage; in the same vein, many clinicians are unaware of impulse control disorders and as kleptomania, pyromania and IED in particular are misdiagnosed as they bear significant similarities to other psychiatric disorders. Therefore, because of the risk of misdiagnosis, the lack of clinician education and patient concerns that may impact patient honesty, a through and efficient psychiatric evaluation and increased clinician awareness is key.

The following criteria are listed in the DSM – 5 for diagnosing Intermittent Explosive Disorder:

1. Recurrent behavioral outbursts representing a failure to control aggressive impulses as manifested by either of the following:

   a. Verbal aggression or physical aggression
   b. Three behavioral outbursts involving damage or destruction of property or physical assault during a 12-month period.

2. The magnitude of aggressiveness expressed during the recurrent episodes is grossly out of proportion to the provocation or to any precipitating psychosocial stressors.
3. The recurrent aggressive outbursts are not premeditated or committed to achieve a tangible objective.
4. The recurrent aggressive outbursts cause marked distress in the individual or impairment in occupational or interpersonal functioning.
5. Chronological age is at least 6 years
6. The aggressive episodes are not better accounted for by another mental disorder (e.g., Antisocial Personality Disorder, Borderline Personality Disorder, a Psychotic Disorder, a Manic Episode, Conduct Disorder, or Attention-Deficit/Hyperactivity Disorder) and are not due to the direct physiological effects of a substance or a general medical condition (e.g., head trauma, Alzheimer's disease). (APA, 2013)

The DSM-5 diagnostic criteria for pyromania are as follows:

1. Deliberate and purposeful fire setting on more than one occasion.
2. Tension or affective arousal before the act.
3. Fascination with, interest in, curiosity about, or attraction to fire and its situational contexts (e.g., paraphernalia, uses, consequences).
4. Pleasure, gratification, or relief when setting fires, or when witnessing or participating in their aftermath.
5. The fire setting is not done for monetary gain, as an expression of sociopolitical ideology, to conceal criminal activity, to express anger or vengeance, to improve one's living circumstances, in response to a delusion or a hallucination, or as a result of impaired judgment (e.g., in Dementia, Mental Retardation, Substance Intoxication).
6. The fire setting is not better accounted for by Conduct Disorder, a Manic Episode, or Antisocial Personality Disorder. (APA, 2013)

These criteria may prove useful for a clinician who suspects their client may have kleptomania. In addition, clinicians may find the Structured Clinical

Interview for Kleptomania a useful tool for assessing patients. The DSM-5 lists the following criteria for kleptomania:

1. Recurrent failure to resist impulses to steal objects that are not needed for personal use or for their monetary value.
2. Increasing sense of tension immediately before committing the theft.
3. Pleasure, gratification or relief at the time of committing the theft.
4. The stealing is not committed to express anger or vengeance and is not in response to a delusion or a hallucination.
5. The stealing is not better explain by Conduct Disorder, a manic episode, or Antisocial Personality Disorder. (APA, 2013)

More information on the diagnostic features of these disorders can be found in the DSM-5 where they are included in the chapter on Disruptive, Impulse-Control, and Conduct Disorders.

Comorbidity

Individuals with impulse control disorders suffer from a number of co-occurring disorders. For those with Intermittent Explosive Disorder, comorbid mood, anxiety, substance use and other behavioral addictions are frequently seen (Sun et al., 2012). In addition, individuals with IED often have co-occurring bipolar disorder which has important implications for psychopharmacological treatment of both disorders. Kleptomania has similar high comorbidity of mood and personality disorders; some research suggests that mood disorders might occur in as many as 73% of individuals with kleptomania. Kleptomania also has higher prevalence in patients with lower IQs or after traumatic injuries, which points to the frontal cortex role in preventing this kind of impulsive behavior, though there is a deficit of research on the physiological processes that are present in kleptomania and other impulse control disorders. Pyromania also has similarly high prevalence rates of co-morbid mood and impulse control disorders. Substance use disorders and anxiety disorders are also highly comorbid with pyromania, present in about 33% of cases. Impulse control disorders show a similar pattern of high comorbidity with psychiatric and affect disorders, substance use disorders as well as with other behavioral addictions and impulse control issues. Though there is limited research on psychophysiology, there is provisional evidence that IED, kleptomania and pyromania all show issues with pre-frontal cortex functionality.

Other Compulsive and Related Disorders

History and Epidemiology

There is significant clinical overlap between obsessive-compulsive disorder and behavioral addictions (J.E. Grant, 2012; Rosenberg & Feder, 2014). Patients and clinicians may mistakenly refer to impulsive behaviors as compulsive or obsessive, and previously clear boundaries between compulsive and impulsive behaviors are now more blurred. Though there are significant similarities, those with a behavioral addiction or obsessive compulsive disorder may engage in a behavior repetitively and be pre-occupied with thoughts of the behavior; the key difference is that those with behavioral additions often feel pleasure when engaging in their addictive behaviors. However, some disorders classified under obsessive compulsive disorder may be more similar to behavioral additions. Included in this category are hoarding, trichotillomania, and excoriation.

Trichotillomania is characterized by recurrent hair pulling and was first described by the French dermatologist Francois Hallopeau in 1889 (Sun et al., 2012). The world trichotillomania is derived from the Greek thrix, hair, tillein, to pull and mania, madness or frenzy. The DSM-IV categorized trichotillomania as an impulse control disorder, but increasing evidence that the behavioral elements of this disorder are more similar to OCD allowed it to be reclassified in the more recent DSM-5 as a part of the chapter on Obsessive Compulsive and Impulse Disorders (Sun et al., 2012). However, though there are behavioral similarities, trichotillomania does not present with the same unwanted intrusive thoughts as in OCD. Additionally, unlike OCD, trichotillomania does not often respond to SSRIs, or response might fail to be maintained (Stein et al 2010). This disorder is reported more frequently in women than men and also more frequent in children, where it peaks at ages 12-13. Overall prevalence estimates are 1.5% of males and 3.4% of females.

Excoriation (also known as skin-picking disorder or dermatillomania) is characterized by recurrent skin picking that results in significant skin lesions (J.E. Grant, 2012). The DSM-5 chose to include this new disorder after reviewing the growing set of scientific literature on the prevalence, diagnostic criteria, and treatment options. Studies show that the prevalence of excoriation is estimated to be between 2% and 4% of the general population. Though many individuals engage in some mild skin picking as a response to stress, clients with excoriation suffer from recurring medical issues and the disorder causes clinically significant distress and impairment.

Hoarding disorder was also only recently added to the DSM-5 (APA 2013). It is characterized by the persistent difficult discarding or parting with possessions, regardless of the value of these possessions. Like other behavioral additions, hoarding can be difficult to differentiate from collecting or personal preference. However, for individuals who hoard, the quantity of their collected items fills up or clutters living areas to the extent that the intended use is no longer possible. In addition to more current research on hoarding disorder, diagnostic specificity was a primary reason for the change creation of hoarding disorder. Previously, OCD was used as a catch-all diagnosis for this disorder, which meant many cases may have gone undiagnosed as hoarding is not always accompanied by obsessive or compulsive behaviors. Prevalence rates of hoarding are estimated to be approximately 2% to 5% of the general population.

Clinical Presentation and Diagnostic Options

Behavioral addictions that fall under the Obsessive Compulsive and Impulsive disorders category are a unique group of disorders that have sparked a continued debate over which categorization best fits the clinical picture of these concerns. Some researchers argue for inclusion in a category of impulse control disorders or behavioral addictions, focusing on the repetitive nature of the behaviors and the pleasure and relief and individual might feel after engaging in the behavior. Others suggest that they are more closely related to obsessive compulsive disorders, though a pharmacological treatment shows that OCD and trichotillomania, for example, do not respond to the same pharmacology treatment. Others suggest their inclusion in an alternative category, such as "Body-focused Repetitive Disorders" (Stein et al, 2010). Overall, the disorders in this category present with repetitive engagement in behaviors despite consequences and reduced quality of life. Continued research into these disorders, specifically with focus on the physiology and neurochemical patterns of these issues, will help continue to clarify the diagnostic picture and improve clinical care.

Trichotillomania presents with recurrent hair pulling, commonly from the scalp, the eyelashes, eyebrows, pubic region, and legs (Grant, 2008). It is useful for clinicians to gain an accurate picture of when and where the hair pulling behaviors occur in order to develop an accurate picture of the individual clients concerns. The following criteria for trichotillomania are laid out by the DSM-5:

1. Recurrent pulling out of one's hair resulting in noticeable hair loss
2. An increasing sense of tension immediately before pulling out the hair or when attempting to resist the behavior
3. Pleasure, gratification, or relief when pulling out the hair.

4. The disturbance is not better accounted for by another mental disorder and is not due to a general medical conditions (e.g., a dermatologic condition)
5. The disturbance causes clinically significant distress or impairment in social, occupational, or other important areas of functioning (APA, 2013)

In addition to the diagnostic criteria, clinicians may want to use the Trichotillomania Diagnostic Interview to help determine an accurate diagnosis (Grant 2008). Another set of diagnostic tools are the Yale-Brown Obsessive Compulsive scale, a 10-item scale used to assess the severity of obsessions and compulsions that has a specifically adapted scale for trichotillomania, or the National Institute of Mental Health Trichotillomania Symptom Severity and Impairment Scale.

Similarly, with skin picking disorder or excoriation, patients will present with a number of skin lesions. This activity may take up a significant amount of a patient's time and require treatment for infection or in serious cases surgery. Specific *DSM-5* criteria for excoriation disorder are as follows:

1. Recurrent skin-picking, resulting in lesions
2. Repeated attempts to decrease or stop skin picking
3. The skin picking causes clinically significant distress or impairment in important areas of functioning
4. The skin picking cannot be attributed to the physiologic effects of a substance or another medical condition
5. The skin picking cannot be better explained by the symptoms of another mental disorder (APA, 2013)

In addition to the diagnostic criteria, a specially adapted version of the Yale-Brown Obsessive Compulsive Scale has been developed for excoriation disorder (Grant, 2008). A patient rated scale called the Skin Picking Impact Scale uses self-reporting to help gain more information about skin picking habits and behavior patterns.

Finally, hoarding disorder has the following diagnostic criteria:

1. Persistent difficulty discarding or parting with possessions, regardless of their actual value.
2. This difficulty is due to the perceived need to save the items and to distress associated with associated with discarding them.

3. The difficulty discarding possessions results in the accumulation of possessions that congest and clutter active living areas and substantially compromise their intended use. If living areas are uncluttered, it is only because of the interventions of third parties (e.g. family members, cleaners, authorities).
4. The hoarding causes clinically significant distress or impairment in social, occupational, or other important areas of functioning (including maintaining a safe environment for self and others).
5. The hoarding is not attributable to another medical condition (e.g. brain injury, cerebrovascular disease, Prader Willi syndrome).
6. The hoarding is not better explained by the symptoms of another mental disorder (e.g. Obsessions in OCD, decreased energy in MDD, delusions in schizophrenia or another psychotic disorder, cognitive deficits in major neurocognitive disorder, restricted interests in autism spectrum disorder).

Comorbidity

Individuals with trichotillomania, excoriation disorder, and hoarding may also suffer from other psychologically distressing concerns. There is a high degree of comorbidity between hair pulling, skin picking and other body focused repetitive behaviors (Stein et al, 2010). There are also high rates of co-occurring mood disorders, anxiety disorders, substance abuse problems, personality disorder and intellectual disability (Sun et al, 2014).

Other Behavioral Addictions

A long list of unrecognized disorders may also fall into the category of behavioral addictions. For example, compulsive shopping, love addiction, tanning addiction, work addiction, exercise and fitness addiction, risky behavior addictions, among others. Many of these disorders fit with the common components of addiction: salience, mood modification, tolerance, withdrawal, personal conflict, and relapse (Rosenberg and Feder, 2014). However, a lack of research prevents clear diagnostic criteria for these disorders. Many are closely linked with other mental health concerns, and like other behavioral addictions considered above, many have high rates of comorbid psychological concerns. Please see the resources section for more information about these concerns.

References

American Psychiatric Association. (2000). *Diagnostic and statistical manual of mental disorders* (4ᵗʰ ed., text rev.). doi:10.1176/appi.books.9780890423349.

Ascher, M. S., Levounis, P., & American Psychiatric Association. (2015). *The Behavioral Addictions* (First edition. ed.). Washington, DC: American Psychiatric Publishing, a division of American Psychiatric Association.

Association, A. P. (2013). Highlights of Changes From DSM-IV-TR to DSM-5. Retrieved from http://www.dsm5.org/Documents/changes from dsm-iv-tr to dsm-5.pdf

American Psychiatric Association. (2013). Diagnostic and statistical manual of mental disorders (DSM-5®). American Psychiatric

Carnes, P. (2001). *Out of the shadows: understanding sexual addiction* (3ʳᵈ ed.). Center City, MN: Hazelden Information & Edu.

Grant, J. E. (2008). *Impulse control disorders: a clinician's guide to understanding and treating behavioral addictions* (1ˢᵗ ed.). New York: W.W. Norton.

Kimberly S. Young, C. N. d. A. (Ed.) (2011). *Internet Addition: A Handbook and Guide to Evaluation and Treatment*. Hoboken, NJ: John Wiley & Sons Inc. .

Rosenberg, K. P., & Feder, L. C. (2014). *Behavioral addictions: criteria, evidence, and treatment*. London ; Waltham, MA: Academic Press.

Sun, A.-P., Ashley, L. L., & Dickson, L. (2012). *Behavioral Addiction: Screening, Assessment, and Treatment*. Las Vegas, NV: Central Recovery Press.

Abuse, N. I. o. D. (2014). Drugs, Brains, and Behavior: The Science of Addiction. Retrieved from https://www.drugabuse.gov/publications/drugs-brains-behavior-science-addiction/preface

Alavi, S. S., Ferdosi, M., Jannatifard, F., Eslami, M., Alaghemandan, H., & Setare, M. (2012). Behavioral Addiction versus Substance Addiction: Correspondence of Psychiatric and Psychological Views. *International Journal of Preventive Medicine, 3*(4), 290–294.

Chapter 2 Resources

This section gives a list of resources for those who wish to seek out more information on the topics presented in the chapter. For easy navigating this section has been sorted specific categories of behavioral additions. Again, when considering the history and changes to the DSM surrounding behavioral addictions, please note that many resources were created prior to the release of the DSM-5 in 2013, as such many references may include incorrect diagnostic information.

Gambling Addition

Printed Resources

The following books/chapters are selections that may help deepen your knowledge of this subject (see complete references for these above under References).

Behavioral Addiction, An-Pyng Sun, PhD
Chapter 3: Gambling Addiction
Behavioral Addictions: Criteria, Evidence, and Treatment, Rosenberg and Feder
Chapter 3: Diagnosis and Treatment of Gambling Disorder

The Behavioral Addictions, Ascher and Levounis
Chapter 5: Gambling Disorder

Impulse Control Disorders, Grant
Chapter 1: Clinical Characterisitcs of Impulse Control Disorders

Online Resources

The main page for Gamblers Anonymous. Contains resources for meeting locations across the US. http://www.gamblersanonymous.org/ga/

An organization that supports the family and friends of a gambling addict: http://www.gam-anon.org/

Association of Problem Gambling Service Administrators (APGSA) http://www.apgsa.org/

Gambling Disorder Criteria
https://www.problemgambling.ca/EN/ResourcesForProfessionals/Pages/DSM5CriteriaGamblingDisorder.aspx

Journal Articles

DeCaria CM, Hollander E, Grossman R, Wong CM, Mosovich SA, Cherkasky S. (1996) Diagnosis, neurobiology, and treatment of pathological gambling. *Journal of Clinical Psychiatry*, 57 Supplement 8, 80-3; discussion 83-4. https://www.ncbi.nlm.nih.gov/pubmed/8698687

Grant, J. E., & Kim, S. W. (2006). Medication Management of Pathological Gambling. *Minnesota Medicine*, *89*(9), 44–48.

Hollander E, Buchalter AJ, DeCaria CM, (2000) Pathological Gambling. *Psychiatry Clinics of North America*, 23(3), 629-42. https://www.ncbi.nlm.nih.gov/pubmed/10986732

Pietrzak, R. H., Ladd, G. T., & Petry, N. M. (2003). Disordered gambling in adolescents: epidemiology, diagnosis, and treatment. *Paediatr Drugs, 5*(9), 583-595.

Yau, Y. H. C., & Potenza, M. N. (2015). Gambling Disorder and Other Behavioral Addictions: Recognition and Treatment. Harvard Review of Psychiatry, 23(2), 134–146. http://doi.org/10.1097/HRP.0000000000000051

Clark, L. (2014). Disordered gambling: the evolving concept of behavioral addiction. *Annals of the New York Academy of Sciences*, *1327*(1), 46–61. http://doi.org/10.1111/nyas.12558

Worhunsky, P. D., Malison, R. T., Rogers, R. D., & Potenza, M. N. (2014). Altered neural correlates of reward and loss processing during simulated slot-machine fMRI in pathological gambling and cocaine dependence. *Drug and Alcohol Dependence, 145*, 77–86. http://doi.org/10.1016/j.drugalcdep.2014.09.013

Online Videos

Problem Gambling – No One Wins
https://www.youtube.com/watch?v=aVzr5UWMvgU

A Problem Gambler Shares His Story
https://www.youtube.com/watch?v=teTN-zkC5Ac

Sex Addictions

Printed Resources

The following books/chapters are selections that may help deepen your knowledge of this subject.

Out of the Shadows: Understanding Sexual Addiction, Patrick Carnes PhD
Sex Addiction 101: A Basic Guide to Healing from Sex, Porn, and Love Addiction, Robert Weiss
Behavioral Addiction, An-Pyng Sun, PhD
Chapter 4: Sexual Addiction

Behavioral Addictions: Criteria, Evidence, and Treatment, Rosenberg and Feder
Chapter 9: Sex Addiction: An Overview
Chapter 10: The Tyranny of Love: Love Addiction–An Anthropologist's View
Chapter 11: Picking Up the Pieces: Helping Partners and Family Members Survive the Impact of Sex Addiction

The Behavioral Addictions, Ascher and Levounis
Chapter 10: Sex Addiction: The Fire Down Below
Chapter 11: Love Addiction: What's Love Got to Do With It?

Online Resources

Sex Addicts Anonymous - https://saa-recovery.org/

Sex Help.com, Recovery Starts with knowledge - https://www.sexhelp.com/

Journal Articles

SEICUS – Special Report, Sexual Addiction and Compulsions
http://www.siecus.org/_data/global/images/SIECUS%20Report%20
2/31-5.pdf

Online Videos

The Cycle of Sexual Addiction
https://www.youtube.com/watch?v=hGeOeISnb6M

Dr. Patrick Carnes, Interview
https://www.youtube.com/watch?v=i1pQfGD_MQI

Boundaries and Self Care for Partners of Sex Addicts
https://www.youtube.com/watch?v=1MpB36JjmV4

We Need to Talk About Sex Addiction
https://www.youtube.com/watch?v=-Qf2e3XZ8Tw

Why I Stopped Watching Porn
https://www.youtube.com/watch?v=gRJ_QfP2mhU

Technology Related Addictions

Printed Resources

The following books/chapters are selections that may help deepen your knowledge of this subject

Internet Addiction: A Handbook and Guide to Evaluation and Treatment, Young and Nabuco de Abreu

Behavioral Addictions: Criteria, Evidence, and Treatment, Rosenberg and Feder
Chapter 4: Problematic Online Gaming
Chapter 5: Internet Addiction Disorder: Overview and Controversies
Chapter 6: Social Networking Addiction: An Overview of Preliminary Findings

Behavioral Addiction, An-Pyng Sun, PhD
Chapter 7: Inherent Addiction

The Behavioral Addictions, Ascher and Levounis
Chapter 6: Internet Gaming Disorder: Virtual or Real?
Chapter 7: Internet Addiction: The Case of Henry, the "Reluctant Hermit"
Chapter 8: Texting and E-mail Problem Use

Online Resources

The Center for Internet and Technology Addiction
http://virtual-addiction.com/
The Psychology of Cyberspace
http://users.rider.edu/~suler/psycyber/

Addiction Recovery
http://www.addictionrecov.org/Addictions/index.aspx?AID=43

Journal Articles

Yau, Y. H. C., Crowley, M. J., Mayes, L. C., & Potenza, M. N. (2012). Are Internet use and video-game-playing addictive behaviors? Biological, clinical and public health implications for youths and adults. *Minerva Psichiatrica,53*(3), 153–170.
ROBERTS, J. A., PETNJI YAYA, L. H., & MANOLIS, C. (2014). The invisible addiction: Cell-phone activities and addiction among male and female college students. *Journal of Behavioral Addictions*, *3*(4), 254–265. http://doi.org/10.1556/JBA.3.2014.015
Kim, Y., Jeong, J.-E., Cho, H., Jung, D.-J., Kwak, M., Rho, M. J., … Choi, I. Y. (2016). Personality Factors Predicting Smartphone Addiction Predisposition: Behavioral Inhibition and Activation Systems, Impulsivity, and Self-Control. PLoS ONE, 11(8), e0159788. http://doi.org/10.1371/journal.pone.0159788

M. D. Griffiths 2000 Does Internet and computer "addiction" exist? Some case study evidence. *CyberPsychology & Behavior* 3 2 211 218. CrossRef

Online Videos

Quitting Social Media
https://www.youtube.com/watch?v=3E7hkPZ-HTk

What You Need to Know about Internet Addiction, Dr. Kimberly Young
https://www.youtube.com/watch?v=vOSYmLER664

Hooked, Hacked, Hijacked
https://www.youtube.com/watch?v=aqhzFd4NUPI

Food Related Addictions

Printed Resources

The following book chapters are selections that may help deepen your knowledge of this subject.

Behavioral Addiction, An-Pyng Sun, PhD
Chapter 5: Eating Disorders

Behavioral Addictions: Criteria, Evidence, and Treatment, Rosenberg and Feder
Chapter 7: Food Addiction: Evidence, Evaluation, and Treatment

The Behavioral Addictions, Ascher and Levounis
Chapter 4: Food Addiction Sugar High

Online Resources

Food Addicts Anonymous
http://www.foodaddictsanonymous.org/are-you-food-addict

Food Addicts in Recovery
https://www.foodaddicts.org/
DSM-5 Feeding and Eating Disorders
http://www.dsm5.org/documents/eating%20disorders%20fact%20sheet.pdf

Alliance For Eating Disorders – Binge Eating Disorder
http://www.allianceforeatingdisorders.com/portal/suggested-readings-bed

Yale Food Addiction Scale
http://www.midss.org/content/yale-food-addiction-scale-yfas

CDC Brief Report on Obesity
https://www.cdc.gov/nchs/data/databriefs/db219.pdf

Journal Articles

Meule, A., & Gearhardt, A. N. (2014). Food Addiction in the Light of DSM-5. Nutrients, 6(9), 3653–3671. http://doi.org/10.3390/nu6093653

Devlin, M. J. (2007), Is there a place for obesity in DSM-5?. Int. J. Eat. Disord., 40: S83–S88. doi:10.1002/eat.20430

Online Videos

How to Get Free From Food Addiction
https://www.youtube.com/watch?v=IWXXvOJ4SKI

Understanding and Managing Food Addiction
https://www.youtube.com/watch?v=4ddOzKpWBFE

Brain Chemistry, Sugar Cravings and Food Addictions
https://www.youtube.com/watch?v=dzeBOR8WvE4

Impulse Control Disorders

Printed Resources

The following books/chapters are selections that may help deepen your knowledge of this subject.

Impulse Control Disorders, Grant
Chapter 5: Intermittent Explosive Disorder: Relationship to Impulse Control Disorders
Chapter 6: Etiology of Impulse Control Disorders
Chapter 7: Assessment of Impulse Control Disorders

Behavioral Addiction, An-Pyng Sun, PhD
Chapter 6: Impulse Control Disorders

Behavioral Addictions: Criteria, Evidence, and Treatment, Rosenberg and Feder
Chapter 12: Compulsive Buying Disorder

The Behavioral Addictions, Ascher and Levounis
Chapter 9: Kleptomania: To Steal or Not to Steal–That is the Question

Online Resources

The Schulman Center for Compulsive Theft, Spending and Hoarding
http://www.theshulmancenter.com/

Journal Articles

Grant JE, Won Kim, S. 2007. *Clinical Characteristics and Psychiatric Comorbidity of Pyromania.* Journal of Clinical Psychology Nov; 68(11) 1717-22

Schreiber, L., Odlaug, B. L., & Grant, J. E. (2011). Impulse Control Disorders: Updated Review of Clinical Characteristics and Pharmacological Management. *Frontiers in Psychiatry, 2,* 1. http://doi.org/10.3389/fpsyt.2011.00001

Grant, Jon E, & Odlaug, Brian L. (2008). Kleptomania: clinical characteristics and treatment. Revista Brasileira de Psiquiatria, 30(Suppl. 1), S11-S15. Epub August 03, 2007.https://dx.doi.org/10.1590/S1516-44462006005000054

Frascella, J., Potenza, M. N., Brown, L. L., & Childress, A. R. (2010). Carving addiction at a new joint? Shared brain vulnerabilities open the way for non-substance addictions. *Annals of the New York Academy of Sciences, 1187,* 294–315. http://doi.org/10.1111/j.1749-6632.2009.05420.x

Online Videos

Curing Kleptomania – Grant
https://www.youtube.com/watch?v=8PnYb_ZvMzU

What is Intermittent Explosive Disorder
https://www.youtube.com/watch?v=zs0JtjqR3dY

Intermittent Explosive Disorder
https://www.youtube.com/watch?v=5WdUWp77i0g

Other Compulsive and Related Disorders

Printed Resources

Trichotillomania, Skin Picking, and Other Body-focused Repetitive Behaviors, Grant

Online Resources

TrichStop: Online Therapy Resources for Trichotillomania
http://www.trichstop.com/

Hoarding Power Point
https://www.adaa.org/sites/default/files/Rabinowitz_134.pdf

DSM-5 Fact Sheet: Obsessive Compulsive and Related Disorders
http://www.dsm5.org/Documents/Obsessive%20Compulsive%20
Disorders%20Fact%20Sheet.pdf
Treatment of Trichotillomania
https://www.ihs.gov/telebehavioral/includes/themes/newihstheme/
display_objects/documents/slides/nationalchildandadolescent/spring2015/
trichotillomania508.pdf

Journal Articles

Potenza, M. N., Koran, L. M., & Pallanti, S. (2009). The relationship between impulse control disorders and obsessive-compulsive disorder: a current understanding and future research directions. *Psychiatry Research, 170*(1), 22–31. http://doi.org/10.1016/j.psychres.2008.06.036

Online Videos

Trichotillomania
https://www.youtube.com/watch?v=FKX79KuDYyY

Other Behavioral Addictions

Printed Resources

The following books/chapters are selections that may help deepen your knowledge of this subject.

Behavioral Addictions: Criteria, Evidence, and Treatment, Rosenberg and Feder
Chapter 13: Exercise Addiction

The Behavioral Addictions, Ascher and Levounis
Chapter 1: Helping People Behave Themselves: Identifying and Treating Behavioral Addictions
Chapter 3: Problematic Exercise: A Case of Alien Feet
Chapter 12: Shopping Addiction: If the Shoe Fits, Buy It in Every Color!
Chapter 13: Tanning Addiction: When Orange Is the New Bronze
Chapter 14: Work Addiction: Taking Care of Busines

Journal Articles

Granero, R., Fernández-Aranda, F., Mestre-Bach, G., Steward, T., Baño, M., del Pino-Gutiérrez, A., … Jiménez-Murcia, S. (2016). Compulsive Buying Behavior: Clinical Comparison with Other Behavioral Addictions. *Frontiers in Psychology*, 7, 914. http://doi.org/10.3389/fpsyg.2016.00914

Horvath, P., & Zuckerman, M. (1993). Sensation Seeking, Risk Appraisal, and Risky Behavior. Personality and Individual Differences. 14(1), 41-52. Retrieved from:http://dx.doi.org/10.1016/0191-8869(93)90173-Z
Roberti, JW. 2004. A review of behavioral and biological correlates of sensation seeking. Journal of Research in Personality, Vol 38(3), Jun 2004, 256-279.http://dx.doi.org/10.1016/S0092-6566(03)00067-9

Online Videos

Addicted to Exercise
https://www.youtube.com/watch?v=1SVh-YOh3uw
Tanning Addiction
https://www.youtube.com/watch?v=G6Jca1pPUUg

What is Work Addiction
https://www.youtube.com/watch?v=lzbEcNt9VQQ

Exercise Addiction
https://www.youtube.com/watch?v=ne4pJ9QZQMM

CHAPTER 3

Intervention and Treatment

Chapter Overview

This chapter will discuss intervention and treatment for behavioral addictions. First, s series of case studies will highlight the widely variable nature of different types of behavioral addictions, and the range of treatment challenges they may present. These are followed by an overview of the types of treatments commonly used in behavioral addiction therapy. Additionally, this chapter will look at differences and similarities between harm reduction based models of treatment and abstinence only models of treatment.

Case Studies

The case studies presented below are offered as a way to begin understanding behavioral addictions in the real world. When presented with each case please consider the following questions:

1. How has this behavior crossed into clinically significant territory?
2. What concerns would I have if I were treating this individual?

3. What would I do first if I were treating this individual?
4. What issues may be underlying or comorbid?
5. How do I conceptualize this behavior on a broad scale within this particular client's life?

Gambling Addiction: Nicole-Adrenaline and Nicotine

Nicle is a 35-year-old Hispanic woman. Clinical interview reveals that she is living paycheck to paycheck despite having a large salary at a private law firm in the area because most of her money is going to a local casino. Nicole admits that while she is at the casino she gets attention from men, an experience she is not used to and that makes her feel "special." She is unmarried and has no children. She explains that she is on a losing streak, but that she will soon get back to winning, because she has great luck, and when she first started gambling she won enough for the breast augmentation surgery she had wanted for years. Nicole has come to therapy to seek help with her nicotine addiction. She has been a smoker for years but has struggled to break the cycle. She notes that it is particularly hard because there is "no better feeling in the world than driving home with a pocket full of cash you just won, smoking a cigarette." Seeking out this feeling drives her to the casino, and to a second pack, almost every day.

Sex Addiction: Paul and Prostitutes

Paul is a 34-year-old Caucasian male. He is married with two young children, both girls. He has sought out therapy because of his struggles with sexual behaviors and he wants to get them under control before his daughters are old enough to understand what is going on. Paul shares a number of different sexual behaviors that he would like to stop including online pornography viewing and visiting prostitutes. Because he lives in a small community, he knows that it is only a matter of time before he is recognized engaging in these activities and he is constantly scared of what would happen if he were discovered. But he feels unable to stop the behaviors on his own, claiming that he craves sexual contact or sexual images and cannot relax until he "gets his fix." Paul also shares history of ADHD and claims that he has always been a very impulsive person.

Social Media Addiction: Hannah Needs "Likes"

Hannah is a 21-year-old Caucasian college student. Intake assessment reveals that her parents have been unable to support her through college and that during the summer she runs a fairly successful wedding photography business that helps her pay her tuition. Her clients find her typically off of Instagram. In previous years, she did not continue photography during the school year, but this year, she is finding it hard to stay off Instagram. Hannah reports feeling successful and important when her photos reach a certain number of "likes" and that her former goal of becoming a veterinarian is no longer important to her. She admits that she is constantly on her phone during class, checking to see if there have been any new comments on her page, and that her grades are considerably worse than previous semesters. She is at risk of losing her academic scholarship if her grades do not improve. When asked about other issues she is experiencing in her life she shares that her boyfriend of two years recently broke up with her, citing that he said she cared more about her phone than she did about him.

Online Gaming Addiction: Rob's Online World

Rob is a 21-year-old college student of Asian descent. Clinical interview reveals that he is a successful student having earned a full scholarship to an ivy league university. While his achievements should bring him a sense of accomplishment, Rob reports feeling depressed all the time and embarrassed that he has never had a girlfriend or had sex. Though he seems to perform at high levels in school, his social skills are under-developed. Since moving away from home, Rob's time has been increasingly consumed by an online game called World of Warcraft (WOW), where he says he has made the best friends of his life. Now, in the third week of his first semester of his senior year, Rob has missed all but one of his classes. He quietly admits that he has spent the time he should be in class sleeping because late night WOW sessions have left him exhausted. When asked, Rob is able to articulate that other aspects of his life are suffering as well – he has lost 10 pounds because he keeps forgetting to eat, and his facial acne, once under good control, has come back due to his poor hygiene habits.

Binge Eating Disorder: Farrah's Food

Farrah is a 45-year-old woman of Iranian descent. Clinical interview reveals that her family immigrated to the United States when she was young, and that her family struggled financially until she was nearly graduated from high school. This meant that there was often not enough food. Now, she is seeking therapy because she has felt like she has spent the last 10 years on a diet without any success. She has steadily gained almost 85 pounds over the past 5 years and though she has tried Weight Watchers, Jenny Craig and other big name diets, she can't seem to keep any weight off. Her husband died from a heart attack 6 years ago and now she is the sole breadwinner for her children, 16 and 18, both of whom are in high school. Since her husband's death Farrah has increasingly used food for comfort and often finds herself intensely sad and craving ice cream, a food she remembers only having once as a child. When dieting, she reports that her grief increases and she returns to her daily ice cream run as a way to self soothe.

Pyromania: Logan's Fire Fascination

Logan is a 9-year-old Caucasian male. Intake assessment reveals that he has had issues with acting out in school for some time and that he has been held back from starting fourth grade because he has been struggling to understand material in school. At home, Logan's parents share that he has repeatedly started small fires with lighters that he steals from his father (a smoker), and plays obsessively with firetruck toys. When he starts fires he appears "messmerized" by them, and fans the flames to see if he can make them spread. He has attempted to go to school wearing his Halloween fireman costume a number of times, each one ending in a screaming fight. Logan was referred for therapy because his teacher heard him talking to another student about how he wants to set his house on fire so that he can watch it burn, and because of concerns for learning disabilities.

Trichotillomania: Harriette's Hair

Harriette is an eleven-year-old Hispanic female who presents with generalized anxiety, wearing a scarf. She is missing eyelashes and her eyebrows are patchy. Clinical interview reveals she has always been anxious in general and last year began to pull her eyelashes out as they "felt funny". This progressed to pulling out the hair on the top of her head as it never looked symmetrical and again, "felt funny". Harriette's teachers have expressed concerns about her work in school as she tends to be very disorganized and that she doesn't seem to make friends as easily as other students. Harriette shares with you that last year her parents began fighting a lot more, and they are currently living separately. This has caused a lot of stress and disruption in Harriette's daily life.

Excoriation (Skin Picking): Catherine's Social Anxiety

Catherine is a 23-year-old female client of unknown, mixed racial background. She is wearing long sleeves and long pants despite the summer heat. Intake assessment reveals that she has significant social anxiety that has prevented her from enrolling in college courses. While speaking about her social struggles, you notice her beginning to pick at a large, raw looking scab on the inside of her wrist. Her forearms have long scratches on them, as if she had drawn them through thorny bushes. With some prompting, she shares that when she feels stress she scratches herself and picks at scabs or bites her nails but does not share more details. In high school, she struggled with an eating disorder, abused cocaine and was briefly hospitalized for suicidality.

Exercise Addiction: Running Into Trouble

Mike is a 32-year-old, Caucasian male. Clinical interview reveals that he has a history of substance abuse that dates back to high school, with serious use starting when he was 18 years old. On his 25th birthday a girlfriend told him that if he didn't stop using she would leave him and that, among other things, pushed him towards getting sober. Soon after he got sober, another friend convinced him get to work towards getting in shape, and in the spirit of self-improvement, Mike signed up for a half marathon in six months. Soon, running became a daily part of Mike's routine. Over the course of a few years, he began signing up for races of increasing distances, often training twice a day for hundreds of miles a week. He started moderating an online runners' chatroom and used his vacation days for work to travel to races. Six months prior to coming in for this session he had slipped while running outside in icy conditions, twisting his knee and tearing his ACL. The resulting break in running, and course of strong painkillers had Mike spiraling, and he returned to running only days after his surgery, going against his doctor's recommendations and seeking out increasingly higher doses of pain meds to get through the day. Now, six months later he has quit his job, increased his training regimen to get ready for another ultra-marathon, and has increased his opioid use to match the near-debilitating pain he experiences in his knee, which never was able to heal properly.

Behavioral Addiction or Lifestyle Preference – Where is the Line?

Though society places a heavy emphasis on research and treatment in the area of *substance use* disorders, *behavioral addictions* in contrast are strikingly under-researched, with correspondingly under-developed literatures and treatments, despite the fact that prevalence rates are estimated to be high in the general population (Grant 2008). One reason for this might be the fact that substance use has direct physical implications, whereas behavioral addictions may not be immediately obvious. The physical implications of substance use (impairment) also have public health concerns such as drunk driving which brings them to public awareness. The illegal nature of many substances might also influence awareness around those concerns. In contrast, behavioral addictions are more often extensions of normal behaviors or needs. This difference is one of the key difficulties of diagnosis and treating a patient with a behavioral addiction: when does the behavior cross the line into clinical significance? *Behavioral addictions as a whole are minimized by the general public as a concern, and even some clinicians and researchers express concern that identifying these behaviors may create "diagnostic inflation"* (Sun et al, 2012). Though prudence is necessary, it is clear that at times, otherwise normal behavior passes into excessive engagement and causes significant distress in the lives of many individuals. As such, it is important to be educated about these concerns and how to recognize them.

Some strategies exist to help identify if a normal behavior has crossed the line into an addiction. First, if the patient continues the behavior despite knowledge of negative consequences and with multiple iterations of attempting to reduce the behavior, they may have a behavioral addiction. Also, keeping in mind the six core components of addiction may also help to determine the clinical significance of a behavior. If the patient's excessive engagement has the following qualities, you may need to consider conceptualizing the behavior as an addiction: salience, mood modification, tolerance, withdrawal, conflict, relapse. Overall, whether these disorders are categorized/recognized by the DSM as Substance Use or Addictive Disorders, or whether they are unrecognized or categorized elsewhere, practitioners and researchers should be prepared with knowledge on how to judge when an interest has crossed the line into a problematic behavior.

Our changing society also has an influence on the prevalence of behavioral addictions and how often normative behaviors may cross a line. Particularly, the advancement of technology may facilitate new forms of behavioral addictions (such as social media addiction) or create newer forms of old addictions (such as online gambling). Also, modern values of consumerism and widespread access to media may influence already at risk individuals as they are constantly inundated with messages about what to purchase, what to eat, how to look and other intense suggestions (these may correlate with compulsive shopping, binge eating disorder, and exercise addictions).

Overall, determining when a behavior has crossed into the territory of a behavioral addiction can be a difficult determination, that requires knowledge of the addiction cycle, assessment of the behavior's impact on a patients well-being, and often, advanced understanding of co-morbid conditions. Consultation is recommended with complex cases and advancing clinical understanding is key.

Etiology and Diagnostic Options

Though some behavioral addictions have been recognized for a long time – pathological gambling and kleptomania have references to them in early writings on psychology in the 1800s – others are more recently recognized concerns such as binge eating disorder and Internet addictions (Sun et al, 2012). This means that there is a huge spectrum of specificity in diagnostic criteria among the behavioral addictions and for some disorders, a large deficit in research that could help solidify diagnostic criteria. While some are recognized formally as disorders, others remain undefined. In this section we will briefly review the etiology theories of behavioral addictions, and then review the diagnostic criteria of addictions and discuss how this can be applied to the heterogeneous category of behavioral addictions.

Though specific etiologies and diagnostic options were discussed in the previous chapter, there is utility in examining etiology of behavioral addictions broadly and considering a framework for diagnosis. A number of advances have been made in recent history about our understanding of the etiology of behavioral addictions. However, much of this research is limited to particular disorders; specifically, pathological gambling has received a disproportionate amount of attention (Grant, 2008). Despite this limitation, a deeper understanding of etiology may be key for correct diagnosis.

Specifically, neuro-imaging and research on neurochemicals have unlocked some understanding of brain activities that match with addictive behaviors. Serotonin and dopamine are the most commonly studied neurochemicals and research suggests that both may play a role in behavioral addictions (Grant, 2008). Serotonin plays a primary role in behavioral inhibition, whereas dopamine is involved in the reward centers of the brain that reinforce behaviors (Grant, 2008). Overall, increasing research on biochemical influences on behavioral addictions will lead to more refined understanding of these issues. Currently, however, the research indicates multiple ways to understand the physiological pathways of behavioral addiction (Rosenberg & Feder, 2014).

In addition to neurology, behavioral, cognitive, and dispositional attitudes may also play a role in the development of behavioral addictions (Rosenberg & Feder, 2014). Many researchers have focused on the role of positive and negative reinforcers in the development and maintenance of behavioral addictions. For example, some point to the pleasurable elements of many behavioral addictions: winning money, accumulating items, eating highly palatable food, having sex. Other researchers highlight that the intermittent reinforcement (such as unknown numbers and timing of "likes" on a social media post) as particularly resistant to extinction, even in the absence of reinforcement over a long period of time (which has significant implications for recovery) (Ascher et al., 2015). Others point to cognitive processing mistakes that highlight successes in various behaviors rather than accurately assessing consequences (as in focusing on winning money in gambling as compared to all of the losses). An additional theory is that a large part of these behavioral addictions are used for tension reduction and affective regulation, a theory that links them closely with substance use disorders.

Personality factors that may predispose an individual to the development of a behavioral addiction are also important to consider when diagnosing and treating a patient (Rosenberg & Feder, 2014). Impulsiveness is a strong predictor for behavioral addiction development as individuals with this personality trait may tend to be highly responsive to positive reinforcement but less sensitive to consequences (Grant, 2008). Other individuals who are highly sensation seeking may look for activities that provide excitement and produce high arousal and avoid more traditional recreational activities. When channeled incorrectly, this sensation seeking can lead to substance use, gambling, and sexual behaviors, among others. Some even argue for formalization of a risk taking addiction disorder.

Overall, it is clear that personality traits, cognitive tendencies, and disposition coincide with neurology to create vulnerabilities to behavioral addictions. Individual clinicians should stay abreast of current research findings in these areas to best tailor their treatments to best practices. Additionally, practitioners need to use this information to help accurately diagnose clients. More research may reveal that this heterogeneous group should not be considered as a group, but rather with different categories. As more research comes to light, the diagnostic picture should become clearer.

As mentioned above, one of the main difficulties of assessing behavioral addictions is that many of these issues are not fully understood or formally recognized. However, though tools may be limited, increasing focus on these disorders, paired with creative clinical thinking, can help improve client outcomes and improve diagnostic quality. In behavioral addictions, information and feedback from the patient, clinician and patient's family/ support network should all be utilized to create a full picture. One specific difficulty in diagnosing behavioral addictions is the shame and secrecy felt by patients. Some behavioral addictions involve illegal activities that clients do not want revealed. Patients may not want to reveal how out of control they feel, and may be embarrassed to share their issues.

For a more specific discussion of the diagnostic criteria for specific behavioral addictions, please refer to the previous chapter. The revised DSM-5 is also a source for diagnostic clarification. The American Psychiatric Association has an extremely useful website on the DSM-5 (psychiatry.org).

From the main page you can access presentations on research used to inform changes as well as documents highlighting the changes for many major disorders.

Harm Reduction or Abstinence Only

Treatment models for behavioral addictions can vary between abstinence based models or harm reduction models (Rosenberg & Feder, 2014). Though this is an ongoing debate in the world of addiction treatment, with behavioral addictions it is particularly complex. Unlike substance addictions, where a client could completely stop using the substance – for example, being "sober" and not drinking – in behavioral addictions, the behavior in question may not be able to be completely avoided and instead it is a certain set of unhealthy behaviors, including types and duration of engagement, that must be avoided. An alcoholic may need to avoid going to a particular bar on the way home from work, and a pornography addict may block pornography websites from their computer. A food addict, of course, cannot abstain from eating entirely, but may need to abstain from certain kinds of food. The abstinence model is used by most 12-Step Programs which focus on the patient avoiding the behavior or substance. However, a weakness of this model is that it is more difficult to achieve, especially with less cooperative patients, and it may be conceptually difficult for behavioral addictions that are necessary or healthy behaviors at lower levels of engagement.

Harm reduction is often presented as a riskier option than abstinence only models, but it may be a needed alternative for some patients with behavioral addictions (Rosenberg & Feder, 2014). For example, in Internet addicted patients, Internet use may be limited to a certain number of hours per day. Social media addicts may visit problematic website but not at a level that interferes with other activities. Food addicts might limit triggering food groups to a once a week treat. Overall, this model tends to focus on progress and patient control rather than complete avoidance. However, some behaviors may be more difficult to put into this model. Many clinicians would struggle with a patient who insists upon continuing to visit prostitutes but who modifies the behavior to reduce the number of times per week to once and agrees to use proper protection (Rosenberg & Feder, 2014).

Common Psychotherapeutic Interventions

A number of specific interventions are suggested for managing clients with behavioral addictions. Many substance use treatment models can be adapted for use with behaviorally addicted patients and their families. In this section we will briefly discuss some of the theories of treatment, options for group therapy, and family therapy. Overall emerging research in this field will help clinicians tailor their treatment for specific client concerns. Though some specifics are discussed here, clinicians should be aware that there are significant limitations in treatment knowledge for behavioral addictions. Many studies have relatively small sample sizes and may involve non-representative samples and outcomes vary across studies in part because what constitutes a positive outcome for a client with a behavioral addiction in itself is up for debate. Many of the resources listed at the end of this chapter may help practitioners to address more specific concerns, and seeking further knowledge as focus on these concerns continues to grow is important for those wishing to stay current and effective.

Motivational Interviewing

Motivational interviewing is often helpful in the early stages of addiction treatment, where high levels of ambivalence are common (Rosenberg & Feder, 2014). This therapeutic technique is a collaborative conversation style that works to strengthen an individual's motivation and commitment to change by exploring the positive impacts and negative consequences of a given behavior. Often, individuals struggling with addiction will have conflicting wants: both wanting to continue their behavior but also wanting to avoid the consequences. Motivational interviewing can help patients clarify their struggles. When utilized skillfully, motivational interviewing can help patients moderate or change behaviors they have previously found difficult to stop, and can also empower clients to make these decisions on their own volition (Miller and Rose, 2009). Ambivalence is not seen as resistance, nor are patients asked to accept that they are at rock bottom. Research on motivational interviewing shows that it can be used successfully to address a number of concerns including obesity, addictions, depression, HIV safety/awareness, among others.

Cognitive Behavioral Therapy (CBT)

Cognitive behavioral therapy is a well-researched treatment option for behavioral addictions (Rosenberg & Feder, 2014). This short term, goal-oriented treatment involves a therapist and patient discussing the maladaptive thoughts of a patient with the goal of then changing behaviors and emotions. CBT has been shown to have positive impact in treating a wide-group of issues including anxiety, depression and addictions. In specific relation to behavioral addictions, CBT can be used to discuss the maladaptive thoughts related to addictive behaviors and creating strategies to compete with these maladaptive patterns (Rosenberg & Feder, 2014). Patients may work to identify patterns of abuse, avoid or better manage high risk situations, and engagement in more positive substitute behaviors (Herkov, 2016). Because this style of therapy is goal directed and requires active participation, clients are often asked to complete homework assignments as part of their treatment process. Some research on problematic gambling treatment with CBT suggests that the disorder may be most effectively treated in individual rather than group forms of CBT (Grant, 2008).

Dialectical Behavioral Therapy (DBT)

Dialectical behavioral therapy (DBT) created by Marsha Linnehan, also may be used as an intervention with behavioral addiction clients. Originally created to address chronically suicidal Borderline Personality Disorder clients, DBT can be adjusted to meet a number of treatment goals and is often used in conjunction with CBT modalities (PsychCentral, 2016). DBT has four main modules and clients learn skills to help manage their lives in each of the modules: 1. Distress Tolerance, 2. Emotion Regulation, 3. Mindfulness, 4. Interpersonal Effectiveness. Adolescent clients are offered an additional fifth module: Walking the Middle Path. In a 2004 study on DBT with modifications for substance use found that DBT reduced alcohol related symptoms by 1/3 and may also prove useful in treating associated issues, including impulsivity (Dimeff, 2008). Further research is needed to determine the efficacy of this treatment for behaviorally addicted clients.

Psychodynamic Psychotherapy

Psychodynamic psychotherapy models may also prove useful in treating behavioral addictions, particularly when done with a relational/interpersonal orientation. This therapeutic model addresses a patient's affect regulation issues and discusses addiction as a failed solution for negotiating conflict around connecting with others (Rosenberg & Feder, 2014). This intervention may challenge a patient to develop a full understanding of how addiction has been their method to avoid the challenges or pain of certain relationships and interpersonal experiences. Clinicians and clients work together to understand the underlying meaning of their behaviors and ultimately to learn to develop more adaptive strategies and coping skills.

Group Therapy and Modified 12-Step Groups

Twelve-Step programs such as Alcoholics Anonymous, created by Dr. Bob Smith and Bill Wilson in 1935, are nearly synonymous with addiction recovery in popular culture (Lancer, 2016). This format has been adapted for a number of behavioral addictions with groups including: Gambler's Anonymous, Sex Addict's Anonymous, Overeaters Anonymous, and Recovering Couples Anonymous (for recovering sex addicts), among others (Rosenberg & Feder, 2014). These programs are based in group therapy, where treatment is characterized by group interactions and activities. Patients in these settings are encouraged to express their true feelings and interactions with other individuals struggling with similar issues is considered key for effective support and encouragement and ultimately, recovery. 12-step programs typically stress abstinence only models of recovery and require strict adherence to program principals and offer participants a large support network. Research on the efficacy of these programs is mixed, although high rates of attendance was linked with higher rates of abstinence, which suggests patients who fully engage in the program will have the best outcomes.

Family Therapy

Like other mental health concerns, behavioral addictions do not only impact the individual but also his or her family and friends. In some cases, family members may be the first to seek treatment because of the negative impacts their loved one's addiction has on their lives. Behavioral addictions impact family members health, trust, finances, and may even have social and/or legal repercussions (Grant, 2008). Despite the negative implications, many people are ignorant about the existence of behavioral addictions and as such do not know to take it seriously or to identify it as a mental health concern. Spouses and family members should be aware that there are options for them to seek treatment, and that early intervention is associated with more positive treatment outcomes. Individual and couple therapy has some evidence of effectiveness in both pathological gambling and sex addictions (research in other areas is lacking). Broader family therapy can be similar to other group therapy work, but with the friends and family of the patient. Some 12-step programs involve families in special meeting that help educate them on how to support their loved one. These models can help engage family members in observing triggers and understanding the cycle of addiction. A great discussion of how family members can respond to various situations commonly associated with behavioral addictions can be found in Grant's 2008, *Impulse Control Disorders.*

Mindfulness-Based Techniques

Mindfulness originated from Buddhist contemplative practice 2500 years ago and has been increasingly integrated into a variety of clinical interventions as a means of addressing issues such as chronic pain, mental health problems, and addictions (Chen et al, 2014). A small but growing number of trails has shown effectiveness of mindfulness-based interventions, which in addiction therapy, are directed towards reducing cravings or the urge to engage in the addictive cycle (Rosenberg & Feder, 2014). As noted above, mindfulness is also integrated into some contemporary psychotherapy models such as DBT. Mindfulness in addiction treatment is meant to help shift client's relationship with discomfort and help promote a non-judgmental stance with themselves and their thoughts. Rather than negative emotions leading habitually to drug use or engagement in an addictive behavior, mindfulness may allow the individual to be more aware of their own thoughts and emotions and interrupt the cycle.

Mindfulness Based Relapse Prevention (MBRP) is a psychoeducational, 8-week, group based intervention that has gained some recent public attention after a 2014 study showed that compared to individuals in traditional 12-step relapse prevention programs, those in MBRP programs for substance use and heavy drinking experienced a significantly lower risk of relapse (Bowen et al, 2014). At a 12-month follow up, study participants who had received the MBRP intervention reported 1/3 less drug use days and a significantly higher probability of not engaging in any heavy drinking as compared to those who had received more typical treatments. The primary goals of MBRP are:

1. Develop awareness of personal triggers and habitual reactions, and learn ways to create a pause in this seemingly automatic process.
2. Change the relationship to discomfort, learning to recognize and tolerate challenging emotional and physical experiences, and to respond to them in skillful ways.
3. Foster a nonjudgmental, compassionate approach toward one's self and one's experiences.
4. Build a lifestyle that supports both mindfulness practice and recovery. (Bowen et al, 2014)

Overall, mindfulness techniques can potentially help clinicians looking to support clients in building their own awareness.

Meditation, Breathing, Self-Control, Situation Awareness

Outside of specific mindfulness techniques, other alternative practices are gaining ground as part of an integrated treatment of addiction. Yoga is a spiritual practice that developed in India more than 5,000 years ago. It aims to help individuals to unite with their core through a series of physical stretches, postures and regulation of breath (Rosenberg & Feder, 2014). Yoga has developed a number of different kinds of practices including transcendental meditation and Sudarshan Kriya yoga. Transcendental meditation is a mantra based technique that strives for a state of alertness with no object of thought or perception (Rosenberg & Feder, 2014). Research on this meditation technique suggests that it may be useful in reducing negative outcomes and increasing self-concept and internal locus of control. Sudarshan Kriya yoga (SKY) is a breathing technique taught by thousands of trained teachers around the world that involves a complex set of breathing exercises. A randomized study done in 2006 compared recovering alcoholics who were taught SKY versus a control group. The experimental group had significant improvements on their scores on the Addiction Severity Index and reported improvements in quality of life. Though there are no direct studies for these alternative interventions with behavioral addictions specifically, findings related to substance addictions can be used to understand how they might apply to behavioral addictions. Further research is needed to determine which specific populations may benefit most from these alternative treatments.

Art Therapy

Because shame and privacy are key components of behavioral addictions, patients may need help sharing their experiences outside of the traditional psychotherapy context (Sun et al., 2012). Practitioners may consider incorporating creative therapy practices such as art, music, dance and drama into their practice. These creative practices have been show to allow patients to explore and express thoughts and feelings in a safe way and allow for exploration of emotions typically associated with their out of control behaviors. For sexual addictions this technique may be particularly relevant as social norms surrounding discussion of sexual acts may make it difficult for clients to share their experiences. Overall, creative techniques have been shown to break down client defenses more quickly with less trauma. These methods could be especially incredibly useful for helping behaviorally addicted clients express themselves.

Psychopharmaceutical Treatments

Though no specific medications are recommended in the treatment of behavioral addictions, some practitioners recommend the use of psychiatric medications to help treat these concerns (Jon E. Grant, 2008; Rosenberg & Feder, 2014; Sun et al., 2012). Medication is often prescribed to treat comorbid conditions, and many are proposing the use of anti-addiction medications such as N-acetylcysteine (NAC), a glutamate-modulating agent that has also been found helpful in trials with substance use disorders to directly treat behavioral addictions.

Other potentially promising medications for the treatment of behavioral addictions are the opiate antagonists that presumably act by interfering with reward center pathways. Though provisional research shows promise in relation to these particular pharmacological treatments, patients with behavioral addictions are currently treated with traditional antidepressants, anti-compulsive medications, mood stabilizers, anxiolytics, and attention-deficit medications to treat specific symptoms; no medications are given for the treatment of behavioral addictions, per se. Concerns for medication management include numerous side effects of the prescription drugs and lack of research into their effectiveness at treating these concerns.

Gambling disorder is one of the most well researched behavioral addictions and as such has a higher volume of pharmacotherapy research studies (Sun et al., 2012). These studies suggest that certain medications may have a beneficial impact when treating gambling addictions. A double blind study done in 2001 showed that naltrexone (an opiate antagonist) demonstrated superiority to placebo in subjects with pathological gambling. However, more than 20% of the study participants developed abnormal liver function tests during the only 12-week long study (Jon E. Grant, 2008). In another study on N-acetylcysteine, a glutamatergic agent, found that it significantly reduced symptoms of pathological gambling in nearly 60% of the patients during the open label portion of the study (Grant, 2008). Overall, these results call for additional research into medical treatments for behavioral addictions, particular those that show long term efficacy and tolerance.

References

American Psychiatric Association. (2000). *Diagnostic and statistical manual of mental disorders* (4th ed., text rev.). doi:10.1176/appi.books.9780890423349.

Ascher, M. S., Levounis, P., & American Psychiatric Association. (2015). *The Behavioral Addictions* (First edition. ed.). Washington, DC: American Psychiatric Publishing, a division of American Psychiatric Association.

Association, A. P. (2013a). Highlights of Changes From DSM-IV-TR to DSM-5. Retrieved from http://www.dsm5.org/Documents/changes from dsm-iv-tr to dsm-5.pdf

Bowen, S., Chawla, N., Collins, S. E., Witkiewitz, K., Hsu, S., Grow, J., … Marlatt, A. (2009). Mindfulness-Based Relapse Prevention for Substance Use Disorders: A Pilot Efficacy Trial. *Substance Abuse, 30*(4), 295–305. http://doi.org/10.1080/08897070903250084

Chen, P., Jindani, F., Perry, J., & Turner, N. L. (2014). Mindfulness and problem gambling treatment. *Asian Journal of Gambling Issues and Public Health*, 4(1), 1.

Dimeff, L. A., & Linehan, M. M. (2008). Dialectical Behavior Therapy for Substance Abusers. *Addiction Science & Clinical Practice*, 4(2), 39–47.

Grant, J. E. (2008). *Impulse control disorders: a clinician's guide to understanding and treating behavioral addictions* (1st ed.). New York: W.W. Norton.

Rosenberg, K. P., & Feder, L. C. (2014). *Behavioral addictions: criteria, evidence, and treatment.* London ; Waltham, MA: Academic Press.

Lancer, D. (2016). Recovery Using the 12 Steps. *Psych Central.* Retrieved on October 1, 2016, from http://psychcentral.com/lib/recovery-using-the-12-steps/

Miller, W. R., & Rose, G. S. (2009). Toward a Theory of Motivational Interviewing. *The American Psychologist, 64*(6), 527–537. http://doi.org/10.1037/a0016830

Sun, A.-P., Ashley, L. L., & Dickson, L. (2012). *Behavioral Addiction: Screening, Assessment, and Treatment.* Las Vegas, NV: Central Recovery Press.

Herkov, M. (2016). About Cognitive Psychotherapy. *Psych Central.* Retrieved on October 1, 2016, from http://psychcentral.com/lib/about-cognitive-psychotherapy/

Psych Central. (2016). An Overview of Dialectical Behavior Therapy. *Psych Central.* Retrieved on October 1, 2016, from http://psychcentral.com/lib/an-overview-of-dialectical-behavior-therapy/

Chapter 3 Resources

This section gives a list of resources for those who wish to seek out more information on the topics presented in the chapter.

Printed Resources
The following books/chapters are selections that may help deepen your knowledge of this subject.

Dialectical Behavior Therapy in Clinical Practice: Applications Across Disorders and Settings, Linda Dimeff and Kelly Koerner
Behavioral Addictions: Criteria, Evidence, and Treatment, Rosenberg and Feder
Chapter 8: New Directions in the Pharmacological Treatment of Food Addiction, Overeating, and Obesity

Internet Addiction: A Handbook and Guide to Evaluation and Treatment, Young and Nabuco de Abreu
Chapter 9: Psychotherapy for Internet Addiction
Chapter 10: Working with Adolescents Addicted to the Internet
Chapter 13: Toward the Prevention of Adolescent Internet Addiction
Chapter 14: Systemic Dynamics with Adolescents Addicted to the Internet

Impulse Control Disorders, Grant
Chapter 8: How to Treat Impulse Control Disorders
Chapter 9: The Role of the Family

Cognitive therapy of depression. Beck

The Feeling Good Handbook. Burns
Online Resources

Addiction.com, Mindfulness as a Treatment for Behavioral Addictions - *https://www.addiction.com/expert-blogs/mindfulness-treatment-behavioral-addictions/*

FDA Safety Alerts - Aripiprazole use in Impulse Control Problems
http://www.fda.gov/Safety/MedWatch/SafetyInformation/SafetyAlerts forHumanMedicalProducts/ucm498823.htm?source=govdelivery&utm_me dium=email&utm_source=govdelivery

Beyond Talk: Learning How to Replace Addictive Behaviors Using Cognitive Behavioral Therapy - https://www.promises.com/articles/therapy/replace-addictive-behaviors-cognitive-behavioral-therapy/

Principals of Drug Addiction Treatment - https://www.drugabuse.gov/publications/principles-drug-addiction-treatment-research-based-guide-third-edition/preface

Mindfulness Based Professional Training Center - http://mbpti.org/

Mindfulness Based Relapse Prevention - http://www.mindfulrp.com/default.html

American Addiction Center – Behavioral Addiction Treatment http://americanaddictioncenters.org/behavioral-addictions/

What is Moderation Management - http://www.moderation.org/whatisMM.shtml

In Depth – Cognitive Behavioral Therapy - http://psychcentral.com/lib/in-depth-cognitive-behavioral-therapy/

The Efficacy of Abstinence Treatment Vs. Harm Reduction - https://www.bhpalmbeach.com/recovery-articles/efficacy-abstinence-treatment-vs-harm-reduction

Mindfulness Based Relapse Prevention - http://www.huffingtonpost.com/entry/mindfulness-based-relapse-prevention-interview_us_5645fd24e4b08cda3488638b

Journal Articles

Van Wormer, K. (1999). Harm Induction vs. Harm Reduction: Comparing American and British Approaches to Drug Use. *Journal of Offender Rehabilitation.* 29 (1/2) 35-48. http://www.uni.edu/vanworme/drugpolicy.html

Miller, W. R., & Rose, G. S. (2009). Toward a Theory of Motivational Interviewing. *The American Psychologist, 64*(6), 527–537. http://doi.org/10.1037/a0016830

Bowen S, Witkiewitz K, Clifasefi SL, et al. Relative Efficacy of Mindfulness-Based Relapse Prevention, Standard Relapse Prevention, and Treatment as Usual for Substance Use Disorders: A Randomized Clinical Trial. *JAMA Psychiatry*.2014;71(5):547-556. doi:10.1001/jamapsychiatry.2013.4546.

Maynard, B. R., Wilson, A. N., Laburzienski, E., and Whiting, S. W. (2018). Mindfulness-Based Approaches in the Treatment of Disordered Gambling: A Systematic Review and Meta-Analysis. *Research on Social Work Practice. 23(3). 348-362.*

De Lisle SM, Dowling NA, Allen JS: Mindfulness and problem gambling: a review of the literature. *Journal of Gambling Studies* 2012. doi:10.1007/s10899–011-9284-7 doi:10.1007/s10899-011-9284-7

Shonin E, Van Gordon W, Griffiths MD: Buddhist philosophy for the treatment of problem gambling. *Journal of Behavioral Addictions* 2013. doi:10.1556/JBA.2.2013.001 doi:10.1556/JBA.2.2013.001

Reims, KG., Ernst, D., (2016). Using Motivational Interviewing to Promote Healthy Weight. Family Practice Management. 23(5) 32-38. http://www.aafp.org/fpm/2016/0900/p32.html

Online Videos

Using Cognitive Behavioral Therapy for Treating Addiction
https://www.youtube.com/watch?v=o3tRAduJQAk

Addiction Counseling for Beginners
https://www.youtube.com/watch?v=FHb3AM6NzP0

12-Step Programs for Beginners
https://www.youtube.com/watch?v=PDcqZ4QaVPY

Alcoholics Anonymous – The Basics
https://www.youtube.com/watch?v=N3MIGrvUNgY

Motivational Interviewing for Treatment of Addiction
https://www.youtube.com/watch?v=OWqDRu45vPk
Dr. William Miller on Motivational Interviewing
https://www.youtube.com/watch?v=2yvuem-QYCo

Other Resources

National Institute on Drug Abuse (NIDA), https://www.drugabuse.gov/

National Institute on Alcohol Abuse and Alcoholism (NIAAA), https://www.niaaa.nih.gov/

National Institute of Mental Health (NIMH), https://www.nimh.nih.gov/index.shtml

Center for Substance Abuse Treatment (CSAT), http://www.samhsa.gov/about-us/who-we-are/offices-centers/csat

Substance Abuse and Mental Health Services Administration (SAMHSA), http://www.samhsa.gov/

Anxiety and Depression Association of America (ADAA), https://www.adaa.org/

CHAPTER 4

Prevention and Community Resources

This chapter is intended to elaborate on the recovery process for behavioral addictions. To expand on that concept, we will consider how to prevent and identify behavioral addictions, how to manage them, what relapse looks like, and finally, how to connect clients with important community resources. More information on these ideas can be found in the resource guide at the end of the chapter.

Reviewing Key Concepts

As this chapter will focus on recovery and relapse prevention, it is important to review some basic concepts. First, let's look at how behavioral addictions are conceptualized. Behavioral addictions have six core characteristics:

1. *Salience* – The behavior becomes the most important activity in the person's life and tends to dominate thinking, feeling, and behavior.
2. *Mood Modification* – The behavior has an emotional impact on the individual and serves as both a source of pleasure and a coping strategy.

3. *Tolerance* – Increasing amounts of the behavior are require to achieve the mood-modifying effects, and there is often greater recklessness and destructiveness along with increase in the behavior.
4. *Withdrawal Symptoms* – There are unpleasant feelings or physical impacts when the individual is unable to engage in the behavior
5. *Conflict* – The relationship/work/school/responsibility conflicts that arise from excessive engagement in the behavior.
6. *Relapse* – Though the individual has attempted to reduce the behavior, there are repeated reversions to the excessive engagement in the behavior. (Rosenberg & Feder, 2014).

As this conceptualization makes clear, there are strong ties between substance use disorders and behavioral addictions, which at times are called "addictions without the drugs." Though clinicians and researchers continue to debate where these disorders should be categorized, and while the group is heterogeneous in nature, there is clinical utility in understanding these issues under an umbrella of addictions.

Behavioral addictions have existed for centuries but are only now gaining attention in media and in mainstream research and practice. The DSM-5 reclassified pathological gambling and moved it to a part of the chapter on Substance Use and Addictive Disorders, a nod to the commonalities between substance use disorders and behavioral addictions (Association, 2013b). However, many of the other behavioral addictions under consideration, including Internet gaming addiction and sex addiction, did not have enough research to merit formal inclusion. Internet gaming disorder was included in Section III, an optional section of the revised DSM-5, in order to encourage increased research in this area. Overall, though behavioral addictions have relatively high rates of prevalence, there is relatively little research on these concerns.

Also important is understanding the increasing knowledge around neurobiology and how it related to addiction (Rosenberg & Feder, 2014). Only recently have we been able to access information on brain processing to a level of detail where neural pathways might be observed. Most researchers and clinicians agree that behavioral addictions stem from a combination of biological, social, and psychological factors. A number of different biological models for how these disorders develop have been suggested, including the Reward Cycle and cellular memory. These can be examined in more detail with resources at the end of this chapter. Overall, research into the brain chemistry of addiction will continue to develop as more work is done in this area. Clinicians should continue to educate themselves as these rapidly developing literatures continue to advance.

In addition to understanding behavioral addictions as addictive disorders, another theme of note is the high comorbidity of these concerns (Jon E. Grant, 2008). Many behavioral addictions are comorbid with substance use disorders, mood and anxiety disorders, or with other impulse control issues. Although the reasons behind overlap are unclear, dysregulated affect is a common psychological component to behavioral addictions (Rosenberg & Feder, 2014). Some hypothesize that the patient's inability to modulate their own emotions leads them to seek behaviors that will help them regulate these negative affect issues. Thus, behavioral addictions may stem from difficulty building healthy habits around coping. Comorbid concerns complicate the diagnostic picture and increase clinical complexity.

Treatment of behavioral addictions is difficult as there is little awareness, relatively few empirical studies, and at times, no diagnostic criteria (Rosenberg & Feder, 2014). However, CBT has been widely used to treat behavioral addictions and other models of substance use treatment are being adapted for use with these disorders. Alternative treatment models are also gaining traction, as mindfulness base practices and yoga are being utilized in treatment. Traditional 12-step programs are some of the best resources for clients, as a number of specific groups already exists (i.e., Overeaters Anonymous, Gamblers Anonymous). For many behavioral addictions, family therapy is also an important component of recovery (Jon E. Grant, 2008). Complicating treatment is that, unlike substance use disorders, total abstinence may be impossible/illogical for clients. Clients and practitioners must work together to create careful plans that will help clients find success; motivational interviewing may be a useful tool for clinicians when defining these outcomes.

Overall Goals of Treatment and Education

Overall, the goals of education and treatment for behavioral addictions are the following:

1. *Prevention* – Ideally, education and awareness of potentially addictive behaviors paired with instruction in prevention strategies will help at risk populations avoid developing a behavioral addiction. Clinical education will help practitioners to identify vulnerable individuals and allow them to educate on behavioral addictions.
2. *Identifying the Problem* – When a behavior has progressed to a clinically significant level, clinicians will identify the concern and begin appropriate treatment.

3. *Managing the Behavioral Addiction* – Though no specific treatments are designated exclusively for behavioral addictions, an integrative and individualized strategy for treatment will be utilized to help clients manage their addictive behaviors. Clients at this stage will work towards limiting the repetitive thoughts, actions or behaviors.
4. *Relapse Prevention* – As a client gains control of their behavioral addiction, they should be encouraged with positive reinforcement and continued treatment for comorbid concerns. This is a continuing process.
5. *Recovery* – The client changes or completely stops the behavior and is in control of their level of engagement.

Preventing Behavioral Addictions

Behavioral addictions are complex to treat, however, they are also difficult to predict and prevent. Because etiological sources are not agreed upon, prevention based on causal factors can be difficult. Additionally, there is a lack of empirical research on prevention strategies that must be addressed. Though it may be difficult, there are some strategies that may be useful in preventing a behavioral addiction before it starts. Many of these strategies are specific to certain behavioral addictions but some general principals remain. Firstly, monitoring at risk individuals for early engagement in behavioral addictions may help catch these behaviors before they progress to clinically significant levels. In this, the high comorbidity rates of behavioral addictions may be a benefit, as many of these clients may already be in treatment for other concerns and well trained practitioners may be able to notice the early signs of concerning engagement in an addictive behavior. Genetic and neurobiological research may help to identify vulnerable individuals before addictions occur. Additionally, general increased education on coping may help to avoid the development of these addictions as maladaptive coping strategies.

More specific strategies also exist for preventing certain behavioral addictions. In addressing pathological gambling, recreational gamblers can be educated in the probability of winning and encouraged to seek help if their recreation starts to get out of control. Education on healthy nutrition and reduced access to highly palatable food may help to address binge eating disorder and other food related behavioral addictions. In preventing Internet addictions, teaching reasonable use and moderation are key. This knowledge based and educational approach is based in part on the assumption that Internet addictions occur due to lack of knowledge about the potential consequences as compared to substance use disorders (Kimberly S. Young, 2011). Because college students and adolescents are often the impacted population with Internet addictions, specific education strategies addressed to this population may also prove impactful. Also, preventing sex addictions may also center on improved education as well as addressing individual client vulnerabilities.

Again, as behavioral addictions often involve normal and sometimes necessary behaviors, identifying when engagement has crossed the line into clinical significance can be difficult. Most researchers and clinicians agree that when a behavior is no longer life enhancing, but rather the sole focus of an individual's life to the detriment of other interest (salience), and when the behaviors carry increasing consequences, then the behavior is no longer just personal preference. Ultimately, some concerning behaviors might be missed because they do not fit cleanly into diagnostic categories. Continued clinical education and awareness will be key for prevention. If preventative measures don't mitigate a potentially addictive behavior, patients may need to pursue other recovery strategies and clinicians may need to determine the severity of the issue more clearly.

Identifying a Problem

Once a behavior has progressed into clinically significant territory, the key step in the road to recovery is identification. As we discussed above, identifying a behavioral addiction is particularly difficult as these addictions build off of otherwise normative behaviors. Many of the abstinence based, 12-step programs emphasize the loss of control and unmanageability of the behavior when trying to define when an excessive behavior has crossed the line into addiction (Rosenberg & Feder, 2014). While healthy enthusiasms add to life, behavioral addictions take away from it, even though momentary please may be felt when engaging in the behavior. Furthermore, those with behavioral addictions are partially motivated by the drive to reduce the mounting tension they feel around the compulsion to engage in the behavior rather than for pleasure alone.

Though focusing on substance addictions, these signs of addiction from the National Council on Alcoholism and Drug Dependence may be useful for clinicians helping patients who may have behavioral addictions. The signs are as follows, with modifications to account for behavioral addictions:

- Loss of Control: Engaging in the activity more than a person wants to, for longer than they intended, or despite telling themselves that they wouldn't do it this time.

- Neglecting Other Activities: Spending less time on activities that used to be important (hanging out with family and friends, exercising, pursuing hobbies or other interests) because of the behavioral addiction; drop in attendance and performance at work or school.
- Risk Taking: More likely to take serious risks in order to engage in the activity of choice.
- Relationship Issues: People struggling with addiction are known to act out against those closest to them, particularly if someone is attempting to address their addiction-related problems; complaints from co-workers, supervisors, teachers or classmates.
- Secrecy: Going out of one's way to hide the amount of engagement in a behavior or one's actions surrounding the behavioral addiction; unexplained injuries or accidents.
- Changing Appearance: Serious changes or deterioration in hygiene or physical appearance – lack of showering, slovenly appearance, unclean clothes.
- Family History: A family history of addiction can increase one's vulnerability to behavioral addictions
- Tolerance: Over time, a person adapts to a behavioral addiction to the point that they need more and more of it in order to have the same reaction. For example, stealing more or stealing more expensive objects.
- Withdrawal: As mood modifying impacts of the behavior wear off the person may experience psychological symptoms of withdrawal.
- Continued Use Despite Negative Consequences: Even though it is causing problems (on the job, in relationships, for one's health), a person continues engaging in the behavior. ("Signs and Symptoms of Addiction," 2015).

Using this list of concerns may help to differentiate between normative behaviors and addictive patterns.

Of course, identifying that a client has a problem is a key step in getting them the help that they need to recovery from their behavioral addiction. Clients themselves may be resistant to discussing their behaviors as addictions because of the stigma they attach with that term. They may also only share some of the details of these behavioral patterns with a clinician for fear of legal or interpersonal repercussions (Jon E. Grant, 2008). Or they may simply not understand that their behavior is a concern that needs to be brought to their clinician's attention. Bringing increased awareness to these concerns will help to ease patients fears around treatment outcomes and heighten practitioner sensitivity to the potential for these disorders.

Managing Behavioral Addictions

Day to day management of behavioral addictions must coincide with effective clinical intervention, and guiding treatment principals for addressing these concerns are inherently integrative. A number of studies have demonstrated the role that negative affect and mood modification play in development of a behavioral addictions. Therefore, one strategy for managing these addictions may be to intervene in habits around affect regulation (Jon E. Grant, 2008; Rosenberg & Feder, 2014). However, what constitutes effective treatment may change based on the type of addiction. For example, while in pathological gambling abstinence from this activity may be suggested, a food addict may cut certain foods from their diet for 90% of the week. Other behavioral addictions have skills and strategies that an individual might learn to help them manage their concerns. For example, someone who struggles with Internet addiction may log the hours they have been online and set the computer to turn off after a certain threshold. Or someone who struggles with compulsive shopping may create a system to manage their money – perhaps limiting spending on their credit cards. Currently, as no specific therapeutic interventions are suggested, treatment tends to be individualized to match a client's specific concerns (Rosenberg & Feder, 2014).

Relapse

When discussing recovery from addictions, relapse is a common concern. However, relapse is often viewed as a failure rather than a natural part of the recovery process. Relapse is an opportunity to learn more about the etiology of a behavior as well as a chance to process triggers and identify affect. Ultimately, however, preventing relapse is key to recovery from an addiction. Terence Gorski wrote extensively about relapse prevention in his 1986 book, *Staying Sober: A Guide for Relapse Prevention*. He developed a list after working with chronically relapsing patients with alcohol addictions. The list, however, can be easily adapted to work with other addictions. For ease of use, the list of warning signs of relapse is available as a pamphlet that can be printed and then carried in a purse or briefcase. This is a great resource for both patients and practitioners. Gorski suggests that relapse is a process, not an isolated event, and as such, when a client and clinician are aware of the warning signs, the process can be interrupted. The phases and warning signs of relapse are as follows:

1. Getting Stuck in Recovery
2. Denying that We're Stuck

3. Using Other Compulsions
4. Experiencing a Trigger Event
5. Becoming Dysfunctional on the Inside
6. Becoming Dysfunctional on the Outside
7. Losing Control
8. Using Addictive Thinking
9. Engaging in Addictive Behaviors (Gorski, 1986)

Gorski categorizes these steps into three broad categories: 1. Emotional Relapse, 2. Mental Relapse, and 3. Physical Relapse. In emotional relapse, an addict is not thinking of returning to previous behaviors, but rather not properly managing their emotions which may set the stage for relapse. Mental relapse is a return of ambivalence around using and finally, physical relapse is return to addictive behaviors.

In order to help prevent relapse, practitioners should encourage their patients to be honest about their ambivalence rather than attempt to "do well" in therapy. Clients may feel concerned about sharing desire to re-engage in behaviors because they worry they will be judged for returning to maladaptive patterns. Also, as managing triggers around behavioral addictions can be difficult if continued engagement in the addictive behavior is necessary (for example, using the Internet for work), additional supports should be put into place. Mindfulness Based Relapse Prevention has been shown to be extremely effective in helping clients avoid relapse (Rosenberg & Feder, 2014). Other relaxation and replacement behaviors can also be taught to clients to help them manage their emotions and mitigate their desire to use addictive behaviors as mood management.

Connecting Clients with Resources

Knowing resources for clients can help connect them with support networks outside of individual session. Here are some general resources for clients.

National Institute on Drug Abuse (NIDA), https://www.drugabuse.gov/

National Institute on Alcohol Abuse and Alcoholism (NIAAA), https://www.niaaa.nih.gov/

National Institute of Mental Health (NIMH), https://www.nimh.nih.gov/index.shtml

Center for Substance Abuse Treatment (CSAT), http://www.samhsa.gov/about-us/who-we-are/offices-centers/csat

Substance Abuse and Mental Health Services Administration (SAMHSA), http://www.samhsa.gov/

Anxiety and Depression Association of America (ADAA), https://www.adaa.org/

Psychology Today - http://www.psycholoytoday.com

National Council on Problem Gambling (NCPG) - http://www.ncpgambling.org

National Council for Behavioral Health - http://www.thenationalcouncil.org

Recovery.org - http://www.recovery.org/browse/phoenix-az/

References

Abuse, N. I. o. D. (2014). Drugs, Brains, and Behavior: The Science of Addiction. Retrieved from https://www.drugabuse.gov/publications/drugs-brains-behavior-science-addiction/preface

Ascher, M. S., Levounis, P., & American Psychiatric Association. (2015). *The Behavioral Addictions* (First edition. ed.). Washington, DC: American Psychiatric Publishing, a division of American Psychiatric Association.

Association, A. P. (2013a). Highlights of Changes From DSM-IV-TR to DSM-5. Retrieved from http://www.dsm5.org/Documents/changes from dsm-iv-tr to dsm-5.pdf

Association, A. P. (2013b, 5/16/2013). Substance Related and Addictive Disorders. Retrieved from http://www.dsm5.org/documents/substance use disorder fact sheet.pdf

Carnes, P. (2001). *Out of the shadows: understanding sexual addiction* (3rd ed.). Center City, MN: Hazelden Information & Edu.

Grant, J. E. (2008). *Impulse control disorders: a clinician's guide to understanding and treating behavioral addictions* (1st ed.). New York: W.W. Norton.

Grant, J. E. (2012). *Trichotillomania, Skin Picking, and Other Body-focused Repetitive Behaviors*: American Psychiatric Pub.

Kimberly S. Young, C. N. d. A. (Ed.) (2011). *Internet Addition: A Handbook and Guide to Evaluation and Treatment*. Hoboken, NJ: John Wiley & Sons Inc. .

Medicine, A. S. f. A. (2011). Definition of Addiction.

Pietrzak, R. H., Ladd, G. T., & Petry, N. M. (2003). Disordered gambling in adolescents: epidemiology, diagnosis, and treatment. *Paediatr Drugs, 5*(9), 583-595.

Rosenberg, K. P., & Feder, L. C. (2014). *Behavioral addictions: criteria, evidence, and treatment*. London ; Waltham, MA: Academic Press.

Signs and Symptoms of Addiction. (2015, 25 July 2015). Retrieved from https://www.ncadd.org/about-addiction/signs-and-symptoms/signs-and-symptoms

Sun, A.-P., Ashley, L. L., & Dickson, L. (2012). *Behavioral Addiction: Screening, Assessment, and Treatment*. Las Vegas, NV: Central Recovery Press.

Chapter 4 Resources

This section gives a list of resources for those who wish to seek out more information on the topics presented in the chapter.

Printed Resources

The following books/chapters are selections that may help deepen your knowledge of this subject.

Internet Addiction: A Handbook and Guide to Evaluation and Treatment, Young and Nabuco de Abreu
Chapter 12: Twelve-Step Recovery in Inpatient Treatment for Internet Addiction
Chapter 13: Toward the Prevention of Adolescent Internet Addiction

Impulse Control Disorders, Grant
Chapter 8: How to Treat Impulse Control Disorders
Chapter 9: The Role of the Family

Online Resources

Understanding Relapse – Gorski
http://www.tgorski.com/gorski_articles/understanding_relapse.htm

National Council on Alcoholism and Drug Dependence – Signs and Symptoms
https://www.ncadd.org/about-addiction/signs-and-symptoms/signs-and-symptoms

Preventing Drug Abuse – National Institute on Drug Abuse
https://www.drugabuse.gov/publications/drugs-brains-behavior-science-addiction/preventing-drug-abuse-best-strategy

Mindfulness Based Relapse Prevention
http://www.mindfulrp.com/default.html

Journal Articles

Duven, E. C. P., Müller, K. W., Beutel, M. E., & Wölfling, K. (2015). Altered reward processing in pathological computer gamers – ERP-results from a semi-natural Gaming-Design. *Brain and Behavior*, 5(1), 13–23. http://doi.org/10.1002/brb3.293

Wölfling, K., Beutel, M. E., Dreier, M., & Müller, K. W. (2014). Treatment Outcomes in Patients with Internet Addiction: A Clinical Pilot Study on the Effects of a Cognitive-Behavioral Therapy Program. *BioMed Research International*, *2014*, 425924. http://doi.org/10.1155/2014/425924

Olive, M. F., Cleva, R. M., Kalivas, P. W., & Malcolm, R. J. (2012). Glutamatergic medications for the treatment of drug and behavioral addictions.*Pharmacology, Biochemistry, and Behavior*, *100*(4), 801–810. http://doi.org/10.1016/j.pbb.2011.04.015

Grall-Bronnec, M., Sauvaget, A., Perrouin, F., Leboucher, J., Etcheverrigaray, F., Challet-Bouju, G., … Victorri-Vigneau, C. (2016). Pathological Gambling Associated With Aripiprazole or Dopamine Replacement Therapy: Do Patients Share the Same Features? A Review. *Journal of Clinical Psychopharmacology*,*36*(1), 63–70. http://doi.org/10.1097/JCP.0000000000000444

Konkolÿ Thege, B., Woodin, E. M., Hodgins, D. C., & Williams, R. J. (2015). Natural course of behavioral addictions: a 5-year longitudinal study. *BMC Psychiatry*, *15*, 4. http://doi.org/10.1186/s12888-015-0383-3

Probst, C. C., & van Eimeren, T. (2013). The Functional Anatomy of Impulse Control Disorders. *Current Neurology and Neuroscience Reports*, *13*(10), 386. http://doi.org/10.1007/s11910-013-0386-8

Gendreau, K. E., & Potenza, M. N. (2014). Detecting associations between behavioral addictions and dopamine agonists in the Food & Drug Administration's Adverse Event database. *Journal of Behavioral Addictions*,*3*(1), 21–26. http://doi.org/10.1556/JBA.3.2014.1.3

Leeman, R. F., & Potenza, M. N. (2013). A Targeted Review of the Neurobiology and Genetics of Behavioral Addictions: An Emerging Area of Research. *Canadian Journal of Psychiatry. Revue Canadienne de Psychiatrie*,*58*(5), 260–273.

Online Videos

Overcoming Addicton – Preventing Relapse
https://www.youtube.com/watch?v=ymNaZHEqirs

Addiction Relapse Prevention Strategies
https://www.youtube.com/watch?v=bYTp8hpSJjY

Relapse Prevention
https://youtu.be/FmjjxdDwOIc

Motivational Interviewing Webinar
https://www.youtube.com/watch?v=utXazhPTHbM

William Miller – Motivational Interviewing
https://www.youtube.com/watch?v=2yvuem-QYCo

Stages of Addiction and Recovery
https://www.youtube.com/watch?v=Zc05OULLN-U

PART II

Internet-Based Addictions

CHAPTER 5

Internet Additions: An Overview

Historical Context and DSM Revisions

The International Telecommunication Union, a branch of the United Nations that is a widely respected source of global data on communications, reported in 2015 that Internet technologies connected approximately 3.4 billion users across the globe (ITU, 2016). This represents a revolutionary change in the way that people conduct their lives on a day to day basis – in 1995 less than 1% of the globe had Internet access. Online video games also appeared in the 1990s and have increased dramatically in popularity and accessibility (Rosenberg & Feder, 2014). With such incredible rise of technology, some have started to ask when usage becomes too much. Internet addictions are an area of growing clinical concern and practitioners must act quickly to educate themselves about these concerns. It is clear that technology moves quickly. The phenomenon of Internet addiction has been noted in many regions around the globe, including North America, Asia, and Europe, with prevalence rates particularly high in certain Asian countries such as China, South Korea and Taiwan (Sun, Ashley, & Dickson, 2012).

The term "Internet addiction" did not exist until the mid-1990s. During the early years, Internet addiction was rare as people had limited access to the

Internet. Today, Internet addiction has come a long way, affecting the lives of people from all walks of life.

The first study conducted on Internet addiction was published in the *Penn State McNair Journal* in 1996. The study was conducted by Steven John Thompson who began his research focusing on the effects of Internet on society. He also researched on the dependency of individuals to the Internet. His research was accepted at the yearly convention of the Association for Education in Mass Communication and Journalism in 1997 but was not presented because of non-attendance. Moreover, there was also no assessment tool developed to determine the addiction level of Internet use at that time. To measure the level of Internet addiction, Thompson repurposed the CAGE substance abuse screening tool and used it to develop an online survey questionnaire dubbed, McSurvey.

In the study, Thompson surveyed 100 people who claimed to have some sort of Internet addiction. In his full paper *Internet Connectivity: Addiction and Dependency Study*, he noted that Internet addiction still needs more research. There are also some discrepancies with the effects of Internet addiction unlike alcohol addiction as the participants felt a new sense of empowerment for learning new knowledge as well as develop new relationships.

The broader category of behavioral additions, under the umbrella of which Internet addictions fall under, has a complicated history of categorization and classification in the DSM. Behavioral addictions is an umbrella term to describe a variety of disorders including pyromania, kleptomania, pathological gambling, trichotillomania, compulsive shopping, Internet addiction and a growing list of other concerns. Some of these disorders seem linked with substance abuse, while others fall somewhere in the impulsive or compulsive spectrum (Rosenberg & Feder, 2014). In the fourth edition of the DSM (DSM-IV), the category of Impulse Disorders Not Elsewhere Classified included: pathological gambling, kleptomania, trichotillomania, pyromania, intermittent explosive disorder, and impulse control disorders not otherwise specified (APA 2000).

During the revision process prior to the publishing of the DSM-5 in 2013, a number of additional disorders were suggested for inclusion with specific attention to Internet use and gaming disorder (compulsive buying, binge eating disorder, compulsive sexual behaviors, excessive tanning, and hoarding were also considered) (Association, 2013). The revised DSM-5 chapter, "Substance-Related and Addictive Disorders," included Gambling Disorder as the single addition in a new category on behavioral addictions. The inclusion of gambling disorder in this section was meant to reflect research findings that gambling disorder is similar to substance-related disorders in clinical expression, brain origin, comorbidity, physiology, and treatment (2013).

Despite much speculation around Internet addictions and their inclusion in the revised DSM-5, Internet addiction did not find a home under the new category of Substance Use and Addictive Disorders. While Internet addictions as a group may also share similarities to substance use disorders, only Internet gaming disorder was included in the DSM as part of Section III. This section indicates only tentative decisions about the disorder and formal inclusion in future revisions is predicated on further study. Much of the current research on Internet addictions is from studies done in Asian countries and further research in the US and elsewhere is required before its consideration as a formal disorder (2013). Many researchers and clinicians also report some methodological concerns with some of the research that exists on this topic. Other Internet addictions or a broader category of these clinical concerns was not included in the DSM. Internet addictions, sometimes referred to as problematic Internet use, are defined by Dr. Kimberly Young as follows:

> *Internet addiction is defined as any online-related, compulsive behavior which interferes with normal living and causes severe stress on family, friends, loved ones, and one's work environment. Internet addiction has been called Internet dependency and Internet compulsivity. By any name, it is a compulsive behavior that completely dominates the addict's life. Internet addicts make the Internet a priority more important than family, friends, and work (Young, 2011).*

Albert's Avitar

> *Albert, 30, found himself struggling to make ends meet after the birth of his second child and after he was passed over for a promotion at work. One night while at home on his computer, he impulsively signs up for a game he'd heard a friend mention at work. In the game, he creates an avatar (a character) that is a version of himself he wishes he was more often – strong, fit, courageous. Soon he goes from playing causally once or twice a week to three or four hours a day. One month later he is playing for full days – 14 hours straight. He begins to start calling in sick from work so that he can play more often without his wife noticing. When playing online, Albert notes that everything seems okay. Though he tries to reduce his online gaming, he cannot go for more than a few days without returning to the game, even though his wife is*

beginning to become frustrated with his habits. A year later Albert's wife moves out, he loses custody of his children along with his job, as his employer becomes increasingly frustrated by him leaving early. It is then that he comes to seek treatment for his self-identified Internet addiction problems.

Under the DSM-5, there would be no specific diagnostic category for diagnosing Albert's particular concerns. However, it is clear that Albert lost control of his Internet gaming habits and that these concerns fit the characteristics signs of addiction. Online gaming became the most important thing in his life, and he used gaming as a way to manage his mood. He also built up a tolerance over time (increasing from casual use to full day use), and suffered withdrawal effects when he discontinued his gaming. Finally, he continued his engagement despite extremely negative consequences in his life. Understanding Albert's issues will help the clinician decide on the best treatment to support him in moving forward and managing the consequences of his behavior. For example, if Albert were treated with medication for an obsessive-compulsive spectrum disorder, the treatment may prove ineffective (Grant 2008). We will discuss treatment options in more detail later, but emphasize the point that proper diagnosis has real-world implications for treatment effectiveness.

Next, consider more specific criteria for Internet addiction. In 1996, Dr. Kimberly Young adapted the criteria for pathological gambling to serve as a set of criteria for use in diagnosing Internet Addictions (Kimberly S. Young, 2011). Her formulation was framed in relation to a set of 8 questions:

1. Do you feel preoccupied with the Internet think about previous online activity or anticipate next online session?
2. Do you feel the need to use the Internet with increasing amounts of time in order to achieve satisfaction?
3. Have you repeatedly made unsuccessful efforts to control cut back or stop Internet use?
4. Do you feel restless, moody, depressed, or irritable with attempting to cut down or stop Internet Use?
5. Do you stay online longer than originally intended?
6. Have you jeopardized or risked the loss of significant relationships, jobs, educational or career opportunities because of the Internet?
7. Have you lied to family members, therapists, or others to conceal the extent of involvement with the Internet?

8. Do you use the Internet as a way of escaping from problems or of relieving a dysphoric mood (e.g., feelings of helplessness, guilt, anxiety, depression?).

Though adapted from the criteria used to diagnose pathological gambling, and not yet recognized by the DSM in relation to Internet Addiction, these criteria help to clarify some of the essential features of problematic Internet use. While the categories continue to be refined, any excessive Internet use could cause intrapersonal and interpersonal problems and might lead an individual client to seek clinical care. Ultimately, the simplest way of understanding the difference between an addiction and a healthy enthusiasm is that healthy enthusiasms add to life and addictions detract from it (Sun et al., 2012). Ongoing attention to these addictions will continue to improve our understanding of these concerns and improve clinical effectiveness in treating them.

Internet Addictions and Substance Abuse Disorders: Are they the Same?

Internet addictions share much in common with substance abuse disorders. In fact, the perception of the severity of the Internet addiction epidemic in China and Taiwan has generated a few phrases, including "digital dope" or "electronic opium," to describe the intensity of the addictive nature of Internet use and online gaming (Ascher et al., 2015). Others have referred to these growing concerns as "The New Opium War". In 2007, it was reported that a thirty-year-old man lost his life following an Internet gaming binge. He had played the game three days in a row in a city in southern China. Though paramedics tried to revive him, he died as a result of the combined effects of exhaustion and water deprivation that occurred during his non-stop gaming. Another young Chinese man died in 2012. He was found with one hand still on the keyboard and the other on his mouse after a 23-hour binge of Internet games. The Internet café owner said that the young man was a regular customer who reserved a station 3 or 4 days a week for 8-hour stints. These cases, though sensational, bring attention to this growing area of clinical concerns and highlight the dangerous impacts of excessive Internet use.

Substance abuse is characterized by the obsession or compulsion to use a substance, particularly where the individual lacks control of the use despite knowledge of negative consequences associated with use. Internet addiction has similar features. Core behaviors shared between the two categories of disorders are listed below:

An urge to engage in a behavior with negative consequences
Mounting tension unless the behavior is completed
Rapid but temporary reduction of the urge after completion of the behavior
Return of the urge over hours, days, or weeks
External cues unique to the behavior
Secondary conditioning by external and internal cues and
Hedonic feeling early in the addiction. (Grant, 2008)

Internet addictions can also be considered using this alternative understanding of addiction psychology and the six following core characteristics:

Salience – The behavior becomes the most important activity in a person's life
Mood Modification – The behavior serves as a way to cope or manage negative affect.
Tolerance – Increasing amounts of the behavior are required to obtain the mood modifying impacts
Withdrawal Symptoms – There are unpleasant physical or psychological impacts of abstaining from the behavior.
Conflict – There is considerable negative impact on relationships and responsibilities as a result of the behavior.
Relapse – There is a strong tendency to repeatedly engage in the behavior. (Rosenberg & Feder, 2014).

Both of these formulations highlight the strong similarities to substance use disorders.

Though provocative case studies exist, and considering these two disorders side by side shows a compelling similarity, the DSM-5 failed to formally recognize a category for Internet addiction. And many researchers and clinicians remain hesitant to recognize Internet addiction as something distinct (Sun et al., 2012). Some are concerned that drawing the threshold too low for consideration as an addiction will mean that engaging in anything desirable repeatedly will be considered an addiction, therefore reducing the meaning of "addiction". As with other behavioral addictions, Internet addictions also are an excessive engagement in an otherwise healthy behavior; in this case specifically, engagement in a new technology is in question. These addictions are similar to the addictions to TV and arcade games of previous generations and concerned reactions to these advances may simply be part of their influence on society. Though differentiating between the features of an addiction and a new life style may be challenging, in clinical application, the clear boundaries may have less meaning for clients who would benefit from reducing Internet use. To ignore Internet addiction's negative impacts on an individual patient for fear that the disorder is not well researched, is to further stigmatize and trivialize their concerns (Sun et al., 2012).

One additional benefit for considering Internet use, and behavioral addictions as a broad category, within the frame of substance use and addictions is that this conceptualization allows for the consideration of client pleasure when engaging in the behaviors (Grant, 2008). Those with online gambling habits may look forward to their next opportunity to engage in this behavior with pleasure and anticipation. Also, neurobiology research on individuals engaging in impulsive behavior shows that the same neurotransmitters and neuro-circuits are implicated in both substance use disorders and behavioral addictions (more on that later) (Sun et al., 2012). Simply put, the same biological drive for pleasure and relief of tension that may push an individual towards habitual drug use can also drive an individual towards the potential for a monetary reward (online gambling) or a sexual encounter (in cyber sexual disorders).

Furthermore, substance use disorder and Internet addictions are highly comorbid. Studies done in Finland and Greece found that cannabis and general substance use were commonly associated with Internet use disorders in adolescents (Rosenberg & Feder, 2014). Heavy drinking also correlated with Internet addiction issues in a study with Taiwanese students. Interestingly, parental alcohol use disorders were also associated with Internet addictions as a secondary concern related to other psychiatric concerns in adolescents (see Jang & Ji 2012). Additional evidence for similarities between Internet addictions and substance use disorders comes from the consequences of these disorders. Financial and relationship concerns are common, as are feelings of isolation and interpersonal difficulties; some Internet addictions, such as cyber sexual addictions, may also result in legal issues

Proposed Criteria for Internet Addiction

Internet addiction follows the same components of other types of addiction. However, recent research has proposed criteria to determine the severity of Internet addiction. The presence of three or more of the following criteria may qualify an individual as suffering from Internet addiction. Below are the proposed criteria for Internet addiction:

- **Preoccupation:** Preoccupation with the Internet is characterized by thinking about previous activities done online or anticipating the next Internet activity.
- **Withdrawal:** Withdrawal due to reduced online activity is often manifested by anxiety, boredom, and dysphoric mood.
- **Tolerance:** This is characterized by an increased Internet usage in order for an individual to achieve satisfaction. Severely addicted patients often require longer Internet usage to feel satisfied with their online activity.
- **Continued excessive use:** Using the Internet constantly results in persistent psychological or physical problems but even if individuals know about these effects, they still continue to use the Internet despite the dangers involved.
- **Persistent desire:** Internet addicts often find themselves having difficulty in controlling their desire to use the Internet. Even if they attempt to curb their activities, they are constantly bombarded with thoughts of using the Internet.
- **Loss of interest:** People who are addicted to the Internet lose their interest on their hobbies. They now derive entertainment purely from the Internet and nothing else.
- **Internet as an escape mechanism:** To escape from the reality and uplift a dysphoric mood, many Internet addicts turn to the Internet as an escape mechanism.

Experiencing the first two criteria (withdrawal and preoccupation) are the tell-tale signs of Internet addiction. The rest of the criteria may or may not be experienced by Internet addicts but the severity of the addiction is often higher among people who experience most of these criteria.

On the other hand, it is also important to take note that there is some exclusion to the criteria. Excessive use of Internet should not be considered as Internet addiction for people who suffer from functional impairment or disability that renders them reliant on technology. Moreover, Internet addiction should not be associated with the excessive use of technology that may accompany occupational duties (e.g., Air Traffic Control).

Causes of Internet Addiction

Internet addiction is not yet listed in the Diagnostic and Statistical Manual of Mental Disorder. Even though this may be the case, it has been formally recognized by the American Psychological Association. Internet addiction is a disorder often associated with the younger generation but this condition, in reality, is not defined by age, ethnicity, gender, education, or income level. There are many reasons why Internet addiction occurs, including the following factors:

- **Comorbidity with other addictions:** Internet-based addiction, according to many researchers, is an extension of other addictions or disorders. For instance, people who are addicted to online gambling are also struggling with gambling problems in real life. This is also true for excessive online shopping.

- **Escape mechanism from stress:** A person's emotion plays an important role in driving his or her addiction behaviors. Internet addiction is considered can be considered as an impulse control disorder and how a person channels difficult emotions often results in finding ways to escape their reality. Internet addiction is a sort of escape mechanism from the real world. Under situations of overwhelming stress, people often turn to the Internet to unwind.

- **Physical and physiological causes:** People suffering from Internet addiction often experiences physiological changes. Brain scans suggest that Internet addiction is associated with dysfunctions in dopaminergic brain systems due to injuries or lesions. On the other hand, Internet addiction also releases high amounts of endorphins which tap the brain's reward system. Once an Internet addict stays away from the Internet, it invokes chemical changes in the brain affecting the mood.

- **Peer pressure:** Social modeling plays an important role in Internet addiction as a behavioral issue. This is very evident among younger people wherein peer pressure and social acceptance is very important in their lives.

- **Depression and anxiety:** People who suffer from depression and anxiety are likely to be predisposed to suffer from Internet addiction. This is especially true if they lack the emotional support that they need. As a result, some of them may turn to the Internet to fill the void in their lives.

The Brain and Addiction – A Very Abbreviated Discussion of Biology

There are a number of different neurobiological models that help explain what might cause Internet addictions, each emphasizing a different part of brain functionality. For the purposes of this text we will review the reward cycle (Rosenberg & Feder, 2014). Overall, this can be summarized by the idea that the human brain seeks to drive us to participate in rewarding activities because this helps us survive. Addictions disturb the natural rewarding cycle and misdirect activity towards destructive patterns. For a broader discussion of brain chemistry in relation to addictive patterns please see the resources listed at the end of this chapter.

Internet addictions have an additional layer of rewards that are part of what might make them addicting. The Internet functions on a variable reinforcement schedule – similar to that of gambling. For example, social media notifications or responses to chatroom messages are unpredictable. Variable reinforcement schedules have been shown to be some of the most persistent types of reinforcement and furthermore, Internet use is often combined with high emotional content (such as sexual stimulation in cyber-sexual addictions, or feelings of belonging with social media and online chatrooms and message boards).

Risk Factors

Anyone can be a candidate for Internet addiction. However, the following risk factors are associated with a greater susceptibility to Internet Addiction.

- **Depression:** Going online can provide a great escape from feeling down and depressed. However, spending too much time online can feed depression as it contributes to the feeling of loneliness and isolation. This is also aggravated when people go to social networking sites and see others in better positions than them.
- **Anxiety:** Anxiety disorders like the obsessive-compulsive disorder can lead people to check their email constantly or engage in compulsive Internet use. This behavior distracts a person suffering from anxiety from their fears and worries.
- **Other forms of addiction:** Many Internet addicts, according to researchers, suffer from other types of addictions like alcohol, gambling, sex, and drugs. Apparently, the Internet provides an avenue for people to extend their addiction through cyber pornography, online shopping, and online gambling.
- **No social support:** People who often do not get adequate social support from their family and peers usually turn to social networking sites, online gaming, and instant messaging to establish new relationships. Once they form a new online relationship, they realize

that they are more confident in relating to other people in the virtual world than in the real world·

- **Unhappy childhood:** Research indicates that people who have unhappy childhood have the tendency to turn to the Internet to feel happy.
- **Less mobility:** People who are less mobile and socially inactive are also at risk of developing some form of Internet addiction. It is therefore important to go out and interact with real people otherwise succumbing to Internet addiction is possible.
- **Stress:** Some people tend to use the Internet in order to relieve their stress but this can be very counterproductive.

Warning Signs of Compulsive Internet Use

Internet addiction is a growing problem, especially among the younger generation. Since access to the Internet is a vital part of modern society and is an important tool for learning, children are especially at risk. However, this does not mean that everyone is at risk of Internet addiction just because they spend too much time online. Internet usage can spike depending on a person's online activity. For instance, a person using the Internet to finish a project or spending most of his weekend chatting with his or her boyfriend from another country are not considered Internet addicts.

Below are some potential warning signs of Internet addiction.[2]

- Loses track of time while online
- Preoccupied with specific Internet activities like social networking, pornography, and others
- Becomes easily agitated when online time is interrupted
- Sacrifices sleep to spend more time on the Internet
- Checks emails many times during the day
- Spends time online while doing chores or homework
- Prefers to spend one's time online instead of being with family or friends
- Creates new relationship with people whom he or she just met online
- Feels anxious whenever separated from his or her computer, tablet or smartphone
- Loses interest in one's hobby and prefers to go online instead
- Defensive when it comes to time spent online
- Sneaks Internet access when doing important tasks

- Physical maladies due to prolonged use such as headache, weight gain or loss, carpal tunnel syndrome, and blurred vision
- Depression and other mental disturbances

Diagnosis

In today's modern society that relies heavily on the Internet, is it right to assume that most people are vulnerable to Internet addiction? The answer is no. While most people use the Internet for a long time, not everyone is, or is likely to become, addicted. It is therefore important to know about available diagnostic indicators that may point towards available whether you suffer from Internet addiction or not.

Diagnostic Indicators and Assessments

There are several diagnostic indicators that may be useful in examining Internet addiction. Diagnostic criteria have widely been used by psychiatrists to evaluate the level of Internet addiction. These indicators address specific areas which include mood modification, salience, withdrawal symptoms, tolerance, conflicts, and relapse. This means that people who are addicted to the Internet focus their entire attention on it, thus affecting their moods and their relationship with people. Below are the different diagnostic assessment tools that may be useful in relation to assessing online addiction.

- **Internet Addiction Test:** The first validated Internet addiction test (IAT) was developed by Kimberly Young. Studies have determined that the IAT is a reliable measure of Internet addiction as it measures the characteristics of online use. It also measures the extent of the involvement of a person to the Internet. She was also the first to develop a way to measure the level of addiction from mild to severe.
- **Chen Internet Addiction Scale:** This diagnostic test is comprised of 26 items that are ranked on a 4-point scale. The severity of Internet addiction is determined on the high total score. This test was used in a Hong Kong study to determine the Internet addiction of the Chinese adolescent.
- **Compulsive Internet Use Scale:** This particular diagnostic test was developed by the researchers from the Addiction Research Institute in Netherlands. They first tested it on more than 400 heavy

Internet users and 16,000 regular users. The test has 14 items and uses a 5-point scale.

- **Problematic and Risky Internet Use Scale:** Developed by researchers from the University of Wisconsin School of Medicine in 2012, this 18-item measure has been validated using the factor analysis. The basis of this diagnostic test is the Problematic Internet Use (PIU) diagnostic wherein the addictive behavior such as controlled fixation, desires, and actions over Internet use were measured.

Self-Assessment Test

There are many studies that are conducted to measure the extent of Internet addiction. While the first to create the questionnaire was Dr. Kimberly S. Young, not everyone has the means to approach a psychiatrist or psychologist to take the test. Fortunately, people who suspect they are suffering from Internet addiction can take the self-assessment test.

The self-assessment test uses a five-point scale wherein you answer a questionnaire and rate your behavior from 0 to 5 (5 being the highest). Each rating is assigned with the level of frequency (0= never, 1=rarely, 2=occasionally, 3=frequently, 4=often, 5=always). Questions include the following:

- How often do you forget to do household chores because you spent too much time online?
- How often do you find yourself staying online longer than what you planned or intended?
- How often do you create new relationship with other online users?
- How often do you prefer the excitement of using the Internet than the intimacy of your spouse or partner?
- How often do people complain about your Internet usage or time spent on the Internet?
- How often does your work or school suffer because of your Internet use?
- How often does your productivity suffer because of using the Internet?
- How often do you check your emails in a day?
- How often do you replace disturbing thoughts with soothing thoughts about your Internet activities?
- How often do you become defensive whenever people ask you about your Internet activity?
- How often do you worry about living a life without the Internet?

- How often do you anticipate the thought of going online again?
- How often do you sacrifice your sleep because of using too much Internet before bedtime?
- How often do you feel angry at someone bothering you while you are online?
- How often do you always tell people that you are just going to use the Internet "a few more minutes" before logging off?
- How often do you feel preoccupied with thoughts about the Internet while offline?
- How often do you feel secretive about how long you have been online?
- How often do you attempt to reduce your online activity but end up failing?
- How often do you feel dysphoric (hopeless, sad or depressed) whenever you are offline and happy once you are online?
- How often do you prefer to spend more time on the Internet over doing relevant things in the real world?

Rating these questions from 0 to 5 and computing the results will help you obtain the final results. The higher the resulting score, the higher the severity of Internet addiction. The severity impairment index is read as (1) **0-30 points:** No Internet addiction, (2) **31-49 points:** Mild Internet addiction, (3) **50-79 points:** Moderate Internet addiction and (4) **80-100 points:** Severe Internet addiction.

The Great Debate of Internet Addictions

One of the fundamental concerns in regards to Internet addictions is, what is the patient is actually addicted too (Cash, 2012)? Is the Internet itself is part of the addictive patterns or does it simply serve as a platform for conveying other addictive behaviors? Is it the particular content, the particular gadgets (a cell phone or laptop for example) or specific software that is the basis for the addiction? For example, is a cyber-sexual addiction an Internet disorder or is it simply an extension of a sexual addiction that is conveyed online? Or consider an individual with an online shopping addiction: does this addiction merit a different diagnosis or treatment than an individual with compulsive shopping behaviors? Some researchers have suggested that there may be two distinct forms of Internet addictions:

1. Specific Internet addiction where the addictive behavior is predominantly focused on a particular application of the Internet

2. Generalized Internet addiction, where there is no such specific focus. (Cash, 2012)

Some suggest that there are even different distinct features – psychological and neurological to each of these two subtypes. Most typical and addictive users of the Internet have more narrow, specific purposes to their use. However, this may be difficult to clearly qualify as many consider "aimless" searching of the Internet a specific activity. Thus, the great debate of Internet addictions is the question of whether or not the addicted individual is addicted to the Internet as a source for gratifying other means or as a medium unto itself.

At this time, the provisional diagnostic criteria for this condition are limited to Internet gaming and do not include general use of the Internet, online gambling, or social media (APA, 2013). Other potential forms of Internet addictions include cell phone addictions, online shopping addictions, online pornography addictions, or just problematic and intrusive Internet use (Rosenberg & Feder, 2014). Many of these concerns are "online" version of other behavioral addictions. Some researchers reject the idea that these addicts are Internet addicts and instead suggest that the Internet provides a unique place for them to engage in other addictions. However, others argue that the Internet provides a unique and often private access point, where compulsive and impulsive behaviors are enabled or even rewarded. For example, someone with a compulsive shopping addiction may struggle online because their web-browser saves their credit card automatically, and they may be able to make purchases with only a few clicks, where previously driving to the store was a multi-step process. Or with a different client who is struggling with anxiety over schoolwork, Netflix might provide a welcome and addicting distraction to the work she needs to complete. Thus, though there are similarities to behavioral addictions "off line," the unique elements of the online addictions require specific awareness and clinical intervention, justifying considering them as a separate category.

References

Abuse, N. I. o. D. (2014). Drugs, Brains, and Behavior: The Science of Addiction. Retrieved from https://www.drugabuse.gov/publications/drugs-brains-behavior-science-addiction/preface

Ascher, M. S., Levounis, P., & American Psychiatric Association. (2015). *The Behavioral Addictions* (First edition. ed.). Washington, DC: American Psychiatric Publishing, a division of American Psychiatric Association.

Association, A. P. (2013, 5/16/2013). Substance Related and Addictive Disorders. Retrieved from http://www.dsm5.org/documents/substance use disorder fact sheet.pdf

Cash, H., Rae, C. D., Steel, A. H., & Winkler, A. (2012). Internet Addiction: A Brief Summary of Research and Practice. *Current Psychiatry Reviews, 8*(4), 292–298. http://doi.org/10.2174/157340012803520513

Grant, J. E. (2008). *Impulse control disorders: a clinician's guide to understanding and treating behavioral addictions* (1st ed.). New York: W.W. Norton.

Kimberly S. Young, C. N. d. A. (Ed.) (2011). *Internet Addition: A Handbook and Guide to Evaluation and Treatment.* Hoboken, NJ: John Wiley & Sons Inc. .

Medicine, A. S. f. A. (2011). Definition of Addiction.

Rosenberg, K. P., & Feder, L. C. (2014). *Behavioral addictions: criteria, evidence, and treatment.* London ; Waltham, MA: Academic Press.

Sun, A.-P., Ashley, L. L., & Dickson, L. (2012). *Behavioral Addiction: Screening, Assessment, and Treatment.* Las Vegas, NV: Central Recovery Press.

Union, I. T. (2016). ICT Facts and Figures 2016. Retrieved from https://www.itu.int/en/ITU-D/Statistics/Pages/facts/default.aspx

Chapter 5 Resources

This section gives a list of resources for those who wish to seek out more information on the topics presented in the chapter. When considering the history and changes to the DSM surrounding behavioral addictions, please note that many resources were created prior to the release of the DSM-5. Complete references to these materials can be found in the Reference section above.

Printed Resources

The following books/chapters are selections that may help deepen your knowledge of subjects in this chapter.

The Behavioral Addictions, Ascher and Levounis
Chapter 1: Helping People Behave Themselves: Identifying and Treating Behavioral Addictions

Behavioral Addictions: Criteria, Evidence, and Treatment, Rosenberg and Feder
Chapter 1: An Introduction to Behavioral Addictions
Chapter 2: Behavioral Addiction: The Nexus of Impulsivity and Compulsivity

Behavioral Addictions: Screening, Assessment and Treatment, An-Pyng Sun, PhD
Chapter 1: Historical Background of Behavioral Addiction and the Trend Today

Impulse Control Disorders, Grant
Chapter 1: Clinical Characteristics of Impulse Control Disorders
Chapter 2: Models for Understanding Impulse Control Disorders
Chapter 3: The Compulsive-Impulsive Spectrum: The Compulsive Aspects of Impulse Control Disorders
Chapter 4: The Relationship of Impulse Control Disorders to Drug and Alcohol Addiction

Internet Addiction: A Handbook and Guide to Evaluation and Treatment, Young and Nabuco de Abreu

Behavioral Addictions: Criteria, Evidence, and Treatment, Rosenberg and Feder
Chapter 4: Problematic Online Gaming
Chapter 5: Internet Addiction Disorder: Overview and Controversies
Chapter 6: Social Networking Addiction: An Overview of Preliminary Findings

Behavioral Addiction, An-Pyng Sun, PhD
Chapter 7: Inherent Addiction

The Behavioral Addictions, Ascher and Levounis
Chapter 6: Internet Gaming Disorder: Virtual or Real?
Chapter 7: Internet Addiction: The Case of Henry, the "Reluctant Hermit"
Chapter 8: Texting and E-mail Problem Use

Online Resources

The American Psychiatric Association has a useful website on the DSM-5. From the main page you can access presentation on research used to inform changes as well as documents highlighting the changes for many major disorders.
http://www.dsm5.org/Pages/Default.aspx

The American Addictions Center also have a useful website with information about behavioral addictions: http://americanaddictioncenters.org/behavioral-addictions/

Behavioral Addictions vrs. Substance Addictions
https://www.psychologytoday.com/blog/addicted-brains/201306/behavioral-addictions-vs-substance-addictions

Journal Articles

Alavi, S. S., Ferdosi, M., Jannatifard, F., Eslami, M., Alaghemandan, H., & Setare, M. (2012). Behavioral Addiction versus Substance Addiction: Correspondence of Psychiatric and Psychological Views. *International Journal of Preventive Medicine*, *3*(4), 290–294.

http://www.ncbi.nlm.nih.gov/pmc/articles/PMC3354400/
Brevers, D., & Noel, X. (n.d.). Commentary on: Are we overpathologizing everyday life? A tenable blueprint for behavioral addiction research: On functional and compulsive aspects of reinforcement pathologies. *Journal of Behavioral Addictions*, *4*(3), 135–138. http://doi.org/10.1556/2006.4.2015.017

Billieux, J., Schimmenti, A., Khazaal, Y., Maurage, P., & Heeren, A. (n.d.). Are we overpathologizing everyday life? A tenable blueprint for behavioral addiction research. *Journal of Behavioral Addictions*, *4*(3), 119–123. http://doi.org/10.1556/2006.4.2015.009

Brewer JA, Potenza MN. The neurobiology and genetics of impulse control disorders: relationships to drug addictions. *Biochem Pharmacol.* 2008;*75(1)*:63–75.

Grant, J. E., Potenza, M. N., Weinstein, A., & Gorelick, D. A. (2010). Introduction to Behavioral Addictions. *The American Journal of Drug and Alcohol Abuse*, *36*(5), 233–241. http://doi.org/10.3109/00952990.2010.491884

Potenza, M. N. (2009). Non-substance and substance addictions. *Addiction (Abingdon, England)*, *104*(6), 1016–1017. http://doi.org/10.1111/j.1360-0443.2009.02619.x
https://www.ncbi.nlm.nih.gov/pmc/articles/PMC2865686/

Potenza, M. N., Koran, L. M., & Pallanti, S. (2009). The relationship between impulse control disorders and obsessive-compulsive disorder: a current understanding and future research directions. *Psychiatry Research*, *170*(1), 22–31. http://doi.org/10.1016/j.psychres.2008.06.036

Yau, Y. H. C., & Potenza, M. N. (2015). Gambling Disorder and Other Behavioral Addictions: Recognition and Treatment. *Harvard Review of Psychiatry*, *23*(2), 134–146. http://doi.org/10.1097/HRP.0000000000000051

Tao, Ran, Huang, Xiuqin, Wang, Jinan, Zhang, Huimin, Zhang, Ying, & Li, Mengchen. (2010). Proposed diagnostic criteria for Internet addiction. *Addiction,105*(3), 556-564. doi: 10.1111/j.1360-0443.2009.02828.x.

Chakraborty, K., Basu, D., & Kumar, K.G. Vijaya. (2010). Internet addiction: Consensus, controversies, and the way ahead. *East Asian Archives of Psychiatry,20*(3), 123.

Cash, H., Rae, C. D., Steel, A. H., & Winkler, A. (2012). Internet Addiction: A Brief Summary of Research and Practice. *Current Psychiatry Reviews*, *8*(4), 292–298. http://doi.org/10.2174/157340012803520513

Internet Videos

An Overview of Behavioral Addictions
https://www.youtube.com/watch?v=PaU5geYu98U

Everything you know about addiction is wrong
https://www.youtube.com/watch?v=PY9DcIMGxMs

Behavioral Addictions for Beginners
https://www.youtube.com/watch?v=_wZk8QxrKDY

Dr. Patrick Carnes – Chemical Addictions vrs. Process/Behavioral Addictions
https://www.youtube.com/watch?v=0mbbcPO8_h8

What role do genetics play in behavioral addictions?
https://www.youtube.com/watch?v=5tpLbNK7n50

Technology Addiction and other Behavioral Addictions
https://www.youtube.com/watch?v=5ycoPFTHnjA

Process Addictions – Part I
https://www.youtube.com/watch?v=djnLz3J2YF0

National Organizations

National Institute on Drug Abuse (NIDA), https://www.drugabuse.gov/
National Institute on Alcohol Abuse and Alcoholism (NIAAA), https://www.niaaa.nih.gov/
National Institute of Mental Health (NIMH), https://www.nimh.nih.gov/index.shtml
Center for Substance Abuse Treatment (CSAT), http://www.samhsa.gov/about-us/who-we-are/offices-centers/csat
Substance Abuse and Mental Health Services Administration (SAMHSA), http://www.samhsa.gov/
Anxiety and Depression Association of America (ADAA), https://www.adaa.org/

CHAPTER 6

Types of Internet-Based Addictions

Chapter Overview

The purpose of this chapter is to provide you with an overview of the various types of Internet addictions. We've mentioned many of them in passing and now we will focus on providing definitions and a brief understanding of each type of addiction. This chapter will also aim to identify key similarities and differences between the disorders and address the concept of clients with multiple forms of Internet addictions as well as comorbidity with other mental health issues.

In this chapter each Internet addiction or group of addictions gets is own mini-chapter with the following sub-sections: 1. History and Epidemiology, 2. Clinical Presentation and Diagnostic Options, 3. Comorbidity. Please refer to the extensive additional resources section at the end of this book for more information on individual Internet additions. In the next chapter you will find case studies for many of the categories of behavioral addiction considered here, please refer to that chapter if you would like to read these cases.

Comorbidity and Addiction

Comorbidity is when two or more disorders or illnesses occur in the same person (NIDA, 2012). These issues can occur at the same time or in succession and comorbidity implies that there are interactions between the disorders or illness that impact the severity of both. Addictions are commonly co-occurring with other mental health concerns, a fact that has been documented in national surveys since the 1980s (NIDA, 2012). For example, with substance abuse, data shows that an individual diagnosed with a mood or anxiety disorder is twice as likely to suffer from a substance use disorder. The trend is likely similar for Internet addictions. In this chapter, we will consider some of the commonly co-occurring concerns with each form of Internet addiction. Continued research into effective treatments will help assist clinicians treating individual patients, as clients often have a complicated mixture of issues presenting at the same time and one issue may impact treatment efficacy of the other.

Co-occurring addictions specifically impact each other in ways that are important for a clinician to understand (Sun, Ashley, & Dickson, 2012). Some additive behaviors will increase together, such as drinking and online gambling. Other addictions will alternate in severity, one addiction blunting the withdrawal effects of another. Sometimes, an addict with complete treatment in one addiction only to engage in a new one. Additionally, addicts will at times use a less shameful form of addiction to mask another: Internet addiction may seem like a safer alternative to a cocaine habit. To summarize how one addiction might influence another, the following five categories may be helpful:

6. *Intensifying* – when addictive behaviors take place at the same time and encourage one another.
7. *Ritualizing* – when one addiction behavior precedes another in a habitual/ritual process.
8. *Numbing* – when one addictive behavior allows for another to occur by reducing distress or anxiety.
9. *Combining* – where addictive behaviors are combined for a particularly potent "high."
10. *Cycling* – when an addict completes treatment for one addiction and replaces it with a new, similarly functioning addiction (Sun et al., 2012).

Comorbid addictions complicate the diagnostic and treatment picture and suggest that treatments that do not address underlying concerns will not be effective in the long term. Careful consideration of the relationship between co-occurring concerns is essential for effective treatment.

Problematic Internet Use

History and Epidemiology

Since its creation, the Internet has become an increasingly pervasive part of the daily lives of individuals. We read books, socialize, learn, play and relax as part of an online world. In particular, recent findings around the preoccupying nature of online gaming and social media addiction are gaining traction, along with general concern about preoccupation and problematic use of the Internet. Problematic Internet use is a general category that refers to what others might call Internet addictions. At times, this category may include Internet gaming or cyber-relational and cyber-sexual addictions, however, these addictions have specific qualities that justify their consideration as separate concerns. Problematic Internet use, then, is not just an overview category but a specific refection of the pervasive experience of the Internet itself with multiple reinforcing agents (Ascher & Levounis, 2015).

There are different categories of problematic Internet use and they can be understood as follows:

- **Cyber-sexual addiction:** Cybersex addiction refers to addiction of online sex and other related activities. Cybersex addicts frequently visit online porn or adult websites to feel satisfied. They also interact with other people who are interested in cybersex by joining sexual chat rooms and using webcams. This particular addiction can cause problems with real life relationships. In most countries, cybersex addiction is considered a crime and is punishable by law.
- **Cyber-relational addiction:** This type of online addiction is all about building relationships online. The relationship built, in this kind of addiction, may be sexual in nature or purely for socializing and networking. The main reason why people get addicted with cyber relationships is because they want to boost their confidence. Cyber relationship addiction is also related to social media addiction. The problem with this type of addiction is that people can lie about their age, gender, marital status, and practically build a whole new identity to attract other people.

- **Information addiction:** This type of addiction refers to constantly surfing the Internet to look for information. This can cause information overload which can lead to damaging effects as most information addicts will spend hours and days online just reading on just about anything under the sun. An example of information addiction is looking up for medical diagnoses online which can lead to people self-diagnose themselves with a certain disease.[3] This then causes them to worry over their self-diagnosed condition. And then they move on to find more information on their perceived illness until they finally diagnose themselves with a cocktail of different diseases.

Outside of the neurochemical cycles associated with our basic understanding of addiction, where the brain's reward network is involved in habit forming around addictive behaviors, individuals with Internet addictions tend to have additional mental health issues that may contribute significantly to a client's struggles (Kimberly S. Young, 2011; Rosenberg & Feder, 2014). For example, some Internet addiction researchers suggest that young people are using the Internet as compensation for self-identity, self-expression and social interaction experience (Kimberly S. Young, 2011). Internet addicts, in general, struggle to form intimate relationships and may use the anonymity of the online world to mask their own insecurities and connect with others in a non-threatening environment (Kimberly S. Young, 2011). Clinicians need to be aware that individuals who struggle to form stable social support networks might be vulnerable to Internet addictions, and also should consider the client's social needs when developing a treatment plan to address addiction.

Clinical Presentation and Diagnostic Options

Like the other behavioral addictions discussed in this book, Internet addictions are characterized by the habitual compulsion to engage in a certain activity, regardless of the associated consequences (Rosenberg & Feder, 2014). Rather than dealing with stressors productively, the Internet is used for self-soothing, and when access is limited there may be psychological symptoms of withdrawal. Again, the Internet is multifaceted and may be reinforcing in a number of areas. For example, an individual may use Netflix to help them relax, while another might use online gambling for a "rush" (Ascher & Levounis, 2015). Regardless of the form that Internet addiction takes, diagnosis can be complex (Young, 2011). The Internet for many people is an essential part of daily life and a constructive tool that has advanced our society. In many ways, the Internet is a benefit to individual clients, who can even access apps for relaxation and anxiety reduction. Identifying when use has surpassed a clinically significant level can be extremely challenging. Furthermore, questions about Internet use may not even be included in typical intake interviews as the disorder currently has little recognition in the broad field of mental health. Diagnosis should focus on how Internet use no longer is something the client can easily control, as well as understanding the individual consequences of continued use, and working with clients to understand underlying issues that may be causing them to seek relief.

Currently, few clear criteria are available for diagnosing Internet addictions which are not recognized as a specific disorder in the most recent DSM-5. As parallels between pathological gambling and Internet addition exist, some of the diagnostic criteria in pathological gambling can be modified to apply to Internet addictions. Some of the following criteria might be helpful for consideration:

- Internet addicts, as compared to other users, demonstrate a loss of impulse control: despite consequences, addicts will continue use.
- Average online usage is excessive and basic tasks are interrupted (for example: sleep deprivation, and then resulting patterns of lateness to work or school, or basic hygiene needs are skipped).
- Client has made several unsuccessful efforts to control, cut back or stop their use.
- The Internet serves as a way to regulate mood.
- The client stays online longer than intended and may lie to others about the extent of their use. (Kimberly S. Young, 2011).

Early research on the prevalence of Internet addictions estimate that nearly 6% of Internet users fit the profile for Internet Addiction, though prevalence statistics vary widely across cultures and also based on the criteria used in the specific research study (Kimberly S. Young, 2011). Another recent study showed that one in eight Americans shows at least one of the signs of Internet Addiction. Higher rates of prevalence have been found among college age populations; potentially explained by their level of access to the Internet and encouraged use. Adolescents are also a vulnerable group for development of an Internet addiction. International studies, which make up the bulk of research on this issue show even higher prevalence rates. One study done in India said that almost 40% of Internet users show signs of heavy usage, with the bulk of that group from young, college-going males. Overall, there are some difficulties in comparing prevalence rates directly as differences in study methodologies may dramatically impact the results. However, though more research must be done on prevalence, most show consistently that college students may be at the highest risk for developing a variety of Internet addiction. Armed with this knowledge, clinicians can include relevant questions about Internet addictions when they are treating high risk individuals, especially those with other comorbid concerns.

Comorbidity

Often, Internet addicts suffer from multiple addictions. Clients with a history of drug or alcohol abuse might identify the Internet as a safer way to fulfill their addictive tendencies and simply switch focus without addressing the underlying concerns (Kimberly S. Young, 2011). Other studies have shown that substance use and problematic Internet use are linked (Rosenberg & Feder, 2014). Multiple addictions mean greater potential for relapse and Internet addictions are especially difficult as usage for work or school can increase temptation to return to problematic usage. Other disorders can also impact treatment outcomes. Specifically, depression and other affective disorders (AHDH and generalized anxiety disorder) are linked with Internet addiction (Rosenberg & Feder, 2014). Though a causal relationship has yet to be explored fully in the research, some research has found that depression is the most influential risk factor for Internet addiction (Sun et al., 2012).

Outside of addiction comorbidity, Internet addictions are often comorbid with underlying interpersonal difficulty, such as introversion and social awkwardness (Kimberly S. Young, 2011). Many Internet addicts are unable to communicate effectively in face-to-face interactions and communicating online may seem safer and easier. Others have limited social support and turn to online communities for connection. A study done in 2003 found that 63% of attorneys polled said online affairs were a leading cause of divorce, and whether an affair is going on or not, preoccupation with the Internet and an online world can lead to disconnection in primary relationships, ironically often the opposite of what addicts sought to begin with.

Ultimately, whether Internet addiction stems from a previous addiction or psychiatric concern or causes them, it is important to screen and treat these concerns alongside Internet addiction in order to improve treatment outcomes and long term effectiveness.

Internet Gaming Addiction

History and Epidemiology

In October of 1958, a nuclear physicist named William Higinbotham created the first "video game", a two-player tennis game intended to liven up the laboratory (Ascher & Levounis, 2015). Long lines formed outside the doors, full of people waiting for their chance to play the novel and exciting game. Though the people in line were not addicts, they certainly illustrate the draw of new and exciting technologies such as online gaming. Internet gaming addiction (also referred to Problematic Online Gaming or problematic Internet gaming or a variety of other terms) is one of the best researched forms of Internet addictions and as a result it is the only form of addictions that was included in the revised DSM-5 (Rosenberg & Feder, 2014). However, it was not included as a formal disorder, but rather in Section III as a Condition of Further Study, as more research is needed before its inclusion with formal diagnostic criteria. Online games have been increasing in popularity since the early 1990s and they now represent one of the most widespread recreation activities in all ages, genders and cultures (Rosenberg & Feder, 2014). Typically, these games do not involve winning or risking money, although certain Internet games may encourage players to access new levels or additional accessories for their avatar, and as such they are considered separately from online gambling. Online games also involve communicating with other players in real time, and choosing to compete or cooperate with the players one might encounter. One specific type of popular online game is the massive multiplayer online role-playing games (MMORPGs) (Kimberly S. Young, 2011).

Significant attention has been paid to the potentially problematic and addictive qualities of Internet games. In part, this attention is due to the large follower base: one of the most popular MMORPGs, World of Warcraft, has over 11.5 million subscribers (Kimberly S. Young, 2011). These games are fantasy role playing games where players create avatars that engage in a wide variety of activities along with interacting with others playing the game. As these activities or goals are completed the player's avatar will "level up" and acquire certain objects or traits that determine social status within the game. Many of these games are persistent, meaning that the world of the character continues to change and develop even when the player is not actively engaged. This creates pressure to stay involved as frequently as possible. Additionally, it is virtually impossible to finish these game, as there is nearly an infinite scope of the game's online world, and interaction with other players is typically a more primary objective than winning or completion. Certain game goals, in fact, can only be achieved by working together in a large, cooperative group (Rosenberg & Feder, 2014).

Though Internet gaming addiction is one of the best-researched forms of Internet addiction, diagnostic criteria remain undefined and as such, estimates of prevalence can vary widely. Large sample studies typically report a prevalence of less than 10% (Rosenberg & Feder, 2014). One study that examined individuals in both the United States and Singapore found prevalence rates of approximately 9%. According to an online survey examining all types of online gamers, the average age of users was around 21 years and the participants were mostly male and single; the majority of gamers spent between 15-27 hours weekly online.

Outside of matching the primary demographic profile, some individuals may be more vulnerable to developing an online gaming addiction. Certain personality factors may predispose someone to Internet gaming addictions; several studies found correlation between low extraversion, low agreeableness, avoidance of social situations, and/or low social skills with Internet gaming disorders (Rosenberg & Feder, 2014). Other research suggests that those who choose to participate in online gaming may find it easier to meet people online and have stronger online social self-efficacy than "real life." Certain neurological profiles may also increase risk for developing an Internet gaming disorder.

Clinical Presentation and Diagnostic Options

From a clinical perspective, the debate surrounding the classification of Internet gaming addictions may have limited utility. Rather, clinicians are invested in determining best practice for their clients, whose Internet gaming habits have become "excessive" and begun to impact important relationships, vocational status, and emotional well-being (Rosenberg & Feder, 2014). Furthermore, questions about Internet use are not typically a part of a standardized intake, and practitioners may be generally undereducated about these potential concerns. Clinicians can expect a clients with problematic online gaming habits to spend most of their time engaged in their game of choice. When not playing they often will be preoccupied with fantasizing about the game, and gaming itself may take on a compulsive quality. Research shows that individuals engaged in online gaming are triggered through similar pathways as a substance abuser (Rosenberg & Feder, 2014). Gaming provides a feeling of pleasure and reward which then encourages repeat use and when use is stopped, there may be intense feelings of inner tensions, restlessness, irritability and moodiness. Online gamers play compulsively to the exclusion of other interests, and this activity has significant consequences for their other responsibilities. Also, clients with Internet Gaming addiction may show somatic symptoms, as excessive game play can result in loss of sleep, missed meals and poor personal hygiene.

As noted above, Internet Gaming addiction was included in Section III of the revised DSM-5 in an optional section addressing prospective disorders for potential consideration is later editions of the diagnostic manual. Early criteria for Internet addictions were adapted from Pathological Gambling Disorder, which in turn were modified criteria from substance use disorders. As it stands, the recommended diagnostic criteria for Internet Gaming Disorder include:

> Repetitive use of Internet-based games, often with other players, that leads to significant issues with functioning. Five of the following criteria must be met within one year:
>
> Preoccupation or obsession with Internet games.
>
> Withdrawal symptoms when not playing Internet games.
>
> A build-up of tolerance- more time needs to be spent playing the games.
>
> The person has tried to stop or curb playing Internet games, but has failed to do so.
>
> The person has had a loss of interest in other life activities, such as hobbies.
>
> A person has had continued overuse of Internet games even with the knowledge of how much they impact a person's life.
>
> The person lied to others about his or her Internet game usage.
>
> The person uses Internet games to relieve anxiety or guilt–it's a way to escape.
>
> The person has lost or put at risk an opportunity or relationship because of Internet games. (Association, 2013).

Though the DSM-5 suggests stipulating the condition as mild, moderate or severe, the number of criteria that must be met for each of these designations have not yet been specified (Ascher & Levounis, 2015). The literature on assessment measures for Internet gaming addiction shows that there are a wide variety of assessment tools, though there is some debate about the validity of some commonly used measures (Rosenberg & Feder, 2014). One of the earliest assessments for Internet addiction is the 20-item Internet Addiction Test/Scale developed by Dr. Kimberly Young in 1998. The Problematic Online Game Use Scale (Kim and Kim, 2010), the Game

Addiction Diagnostic Scale (Lee and Han,2007), and the Problematic Online Gaming Questionnaire (Dementrovics et al.,2012) show the most robust psychometric characteristics and may be useful resources to assist with diagnosis and to track therapeutic gains across the course of treatment.

Signs of Internet Gaming Addiction

There are many signs and symptoms of online gaming addiction. Below are some of the signs of Internet gaming addiction.

- An Internet gaming addict does not leave his or her room for days and they are busy playing online games all the time.
- An Internet addict pays little attention to his or her hygiene. All they care about is to play online games all day long.
- Most Internet gaming addicts are at high risk of taking stimulant drugs, so that they can stay awake for long periods of time to play online games.
- They opt to spend more time in the virtual world than with people in real life. Internet addicts refuse to participate in different events that will lessen their time in playing online games.

Comorbidity

Internet gaming addiction is strongly correlated with a number of other concerns. Some research suggests higher prevalence rates of obsessive-compulsive disorder, hypomania, certain personality disorders among gaming addicted individuals (Ascher & Levounis, 2015). Other mental health concerns, such as depression, were also comorbid concerns in a number of studies (Rosenberg & Feder, 2014). Depressive symptoms may be related to excessive gaming and it is currently unclear whether online gaming is the reason for, or the consequence of, co-occurring concerns. However, some longitudinal studies suggest that the causal relationship between depressive symptoms, social phobia and problematic gaming is reciprocal in nature. Internet gaming addicts are also twice as likely to be diagnosed with some kind of attention deficit disorder than those who play recreationally.

Cyber Relational Addictions: Problematic Social Media, Texting and Email Use

History and Epidemiology

In this section we will discuss social media, texting and email addictions, which fall under the general category of cyber-relational addictions according to Griffiths (2000). Though some researchers categorize these into different areas, they are joined by common user motivations (communication), treatments, and patterns of comorbidity. Therefore, we will consider them in one large group. Desire for social connection is elemental to the human species, and some suggest that participation in cyber-relational activities may be driven by these basic evolutionary needs (Rosenberg & Feder, 2014).

The surge of accessibility in personal computers and cell phones has dramatically increased their popularity and changed the way that we communicate (Ascher & Levounis, 2015). Chats, tweets, snapchats, texts and emails are part of life on a daily basis and an international scale. Many people have found close friends, rekindled old flames, or even met their spouses through connections formed online. Social media websites are one of the most common daily uses of the Internet – not only for adults, but also for children and adolescents (O'Keeffe, 2011). Social media is any website that allows social interaction, such as Facebook and Twitter. But the category may be expanded to include some virtual world games like Second Life or the Sims where interaction with other players is the primary game play, or even video websites such as YouTube (others may argue that virtual world games fit more neatly into the category of problematic Internet gaming). Typically, however, these websites involve three main qualities:

1. Individuals construct a public or semi-public profile within the bounds of the existing system.
2. Users articulate a list of the other users with whom they share connection, often in a public way.
3. The system allows users to view their list of connections and also the connections made by other users. (Rosenberg & Feder, 2014).

Research has shown that social media engagement can be positive, offering a place to connect, and that these websites may play an important role in increasing technical abilities and computer savvy for children and adolescents (O'Keeffe, 2011). However, there are also concerns about problematic levels of use and the risks of engaging with others in an online world where there is at times little regulation, with content accessible that may not be age-appropriate.

Parents may be less knowledgeable about the most recent technologies, which may increase the difficulty of proper regulation, especially when it is teenagers and students that make up the largest user base of social media websites (Rosenberg & Feder, 2014).

Problematic email and texting share features with social media. They are both means of connecting with others through a virtual medium, and they both have also been identified as potential areas of problematic Internet use in various parts of the literature (Ascher & Levounis, 2015). Email and texting are both electronic, private and text-based modes of communication. They also are asynchronous, which means that the respondent can take time reflecting before responding, and their discreetness may allow communication to continue in settings where verbal conversations might be considered inappropriate. Typically, text messages are shorter than emails, and the location of use may differ for some users (with texting typically occurring on a mobile phone and email often on a computer), though advances in smartphones and other technologies have blurred these distinctions.

Because of the relative newness of many of these technologies, research has not yet caught up with them and prevalence rates of problematic use are largely unknown. Provisional findings help provide a perspective on the potential for problematic use and the ubiquitous nature of these technologies in our current society. One study in 2006 found that 34% of people reported checking their email every 15 minutes or less, and a 2007 study done via survey of AOL users, 15% self-reported as email addicts (Ascher & Levounis, 2015). A 2012, self-reporting study found that a third of respondents felt that they used social networking websites too often, and other similar studies also found high rates of concern among respondents (Rosenberg & Feder, 2014). However, it is important to remember that the frequency of usage and addiction are not synonymous, and clinicians should take care to consider what negative impacts the behavior may have. Today, smartphones often can be set up to alert users to incoming emails, allowing for constant connection to inboxes. Most people with smartphones also are connected wirelessly to social media networks and receive similar emails from these websites about updated content. A 2008 study showed that there may be gendered differences around email and texting, with women typically sending more messages, and men engaging in messaging during more dangerous situations (such as driving).

Overall, excessive use of these means of communication may be a concern for many users. As with other behavioral addictions, there is some debate about whether excessive engagement in cyber-relational activities should be considered a genuine addiction, and concern about how treatment will occur if abstinence is not a reasonable option. Overall, more research is needed to help further understand this growing area of clinical concerns.

Clinical Presentation and Diagnostic Options

The symptoms of problematic social media, texting, and email use have been adapted from criteria established for substance use and gambling disorders as the DSM does not currently recognize formal criteria for these concerns (Ascher & Levounis, 2015). One way of understanding cyber-relational addictions is in relation to the core components of any addiction. These include:

> *Salience* – Social networking, texting or email becomes the single most important activity in a person life and dominates their thinking and emotional experiences.
>
> *Mood modification* – Some individuals report feeling a buzz or a high, while others feel a sense of escape when engaging in cyber relational activities, and as such, these technologies can be seen as a coping strategy.
>
> *Tolerance* – Typically problematic users have increased their participation gradually, but consistently require more time online to fill their emotional needs.
>
> *Withdrawal Symptoms* – Significant negative emotion can result from disconnection to online social networks. Some research discusses a phantom cell phone vibration, when an individual imagines feeling their cell phone ring despite not currently having it in their pocket. (Deb, 2015)
>
> *Conflict* – There may be interpersonal, vocational or intrapsychic conflict that result from excessive engagement in social media.
>
> *Relapse* – If the individual is able to suspend use, often level of use returns to previous height quickly, even if the person would prefer to stay offline. (Rosenberg & Feder, 2014).

Other clinical symptoms include significant sleep disturbances, disruptions in ability to work, and reduced ability to meet people (in person) and maintain a satisfying social life. Certain assessments have been modified to assist clinicians in "diagnosing" cyber relational addictions. The Internet Addiction Test that is used to assess Internet Addiction may be used to indicate overall problematic Internet use, and the Bergen Facebook Addiction Scale may also prove useful in certain contexts.

Research supports the idea that some individuals may be more at risk for developing a cyber-relational or social media addiction. As noted above, there are some gender differences with cyber relational addictions. Women are more likely to use these platforms at excessive levels, whereas men are more likely to use these technologies in risky contexts (Rosenberg & Feder, 2014). A recent study showed that individuals with strong orientation towards social comparison, those who perceived strong social support through social networking websites, or those who may have a history of difficulty with self-regulation, may be at higher risk for social media dependency (Burnell & Kuther, 2016). Other research suggests that those with narcissistic tendencies may also be at higher risk, as content shared on social networking platforms is typically more self-focused than normal in person conversations (Rosenberg & Feder, 2014).

Social Networking Addiction

Social networking sites can be highly addictive. In fact, the leading social networking website, Facebook, is one of the most addicting websites. Social networking addiction is defined as an addiction characterized by a person spending too much time on social networking sites such that it interferes with the other aspects of their lives.

Although this condition is not officially recognized as a disorder or disease, the behaviors associated with excessive use of social networking sites is not something that should be dismissed. Just like other forms of addiction, social networking addiction is characterized by a set of compulsive behavior that leads to a set of negative effects.

A social networking addict is someone who's constantly checking their Facebook status or checking their network feeds for hours on end. In a study conducted by researchers from the Chicago University, they have found that addiction to social media might be stronger than to alcohol or cigarettes. The researchers scanned the brains of people to see what happens when they talk about themselves which is what most people do in social networking sites. Researchers found that partaking in activities in social media stimulates the pleasure centers of the brain in ways that approximate the stimulation provided by the use of substances.

Signs and Symptoms of Social Media Addiction

Just like other forms of addiction, people who are social media addicts cannot control their compulsion when it comes to NOT using their favorite social networking sites. Below are some of the signs and symptoms of social media addiction.

- **Spending more time in social media sites:** Healthy social media browsing is limited to perhaps an hour or so per day. If you spend considerably more time on social media sites, then you may be addicted yo it.

- **Checking your social media accounts constantly:** Many people carry their social networking apps on their phones or tablets and they constantly check their accounts for any updates. They cannot help checking their social media posts, profiles, and feeds to see if they have new comments, visits, likes, or messages to read.
- **Sharing too much personal information online:** Many social media addicts tend to share too much of their personal information online. These include their photos, locations, and even current activities to gain approval from their virtual peers. Social affirmation is very important for social media addicts. Thus, they do whatever it takes to get it, including sharing crucial information about their lives.
- **Interference with work or school:** Spending too much time on social networking sites can result in reduction of work and school performance. Most social media addicts spend too many hours checking their social media accounts for updates. Over-reliance in social media to build virtual social relationships can cause problems, particularly in real-life relationships.
- **Loss of interest in the real world:** A social media addict tends to lose interest in the real world. They stop engaging in their hobbies that they used to enjoy. They begin to think that their entire lives revolve around social networking.
- **Constantly reporting on social media, even the most mundane events:** For the sake of updating their social media accounts, many social media addicts update their newsfeeds with the most mundane events. This tendency to report almost everything that they are doing is a sign that they are looking for online affirmation. The more likes and comments they get from posting something on their social media accounts, the happier they become.
- **Lack of sleep:** Because of their incessant need to feed their compulsion, many social media addicts are at risk of losing sleeping time because they stay up late just to check what's on their newsfeed. Moreover, the first thing they do after waking up early in the morning is to check their social media updates.

Effects of Social Media Addiction

Social media addiction can become a serious problem. With the popularity of social networking sites like Facebook, Twitter and Instagram, people can become compulsive users of social media. Addiction to social media can lead to many problems. Below are the negative effects of social media addiction.

- **Wasting time:** Social media provides a distraction to people. Social media addicts who spend most of their time checking their social networking stats end up wasting much of their time. Thus, they tend to fail to do important tasks at work or at school.
- **Reduced self-esteem:** Researchers have found that people who are addicted to social media have lowered self-esteem. Their pursuit of social affirmation feeds their self-esteem. However, this does not last long and they often experience a letdown when the affirmation fades.
- **Being vulnerable to predators:** Predators, particularly sexual predators and thieves, are abundant on social networking sites. Since social media addicts share information and photos about themselves, these predators can steal important information for their own benefit.

Cellphone Addiction

Also, called smartphone addiction, cellphone addiction is fueled by the Internet. In fact, researchers view cellphone addiction as the main reason why people suffer from Internet compulsion problems.

An average person spends at least 3.5 hours each day on their mobile devices to do many things such as checking emails and social media, using apps, and watching videos. However, smartphone addicts spend more time on their phones than anything else which can cause them to neglect their real life relationships.

Why Are Mobile Phones So Addictive?

There is an increasing number of people who are addicted to mobile phones. It is estimated that 40% of healthy Americans are addicted to their mobile phones. Mobile phone addiction has given birth to a new kind of phobia called *nomophobia* which is the fear of being without a mobile phone. But what makes mobile phones so addictive?

One of the reasons why smartphones are so addictive is that they stimulate the release of dopamine. The brain releases a neurotransmitter called dopamine which creates a feel-good sensation while one is using his or her smartphone. Dopamine motivates the pleasure center of the brain. Thus, if a mobile phone addict uses his or her phone, it activates the release of such neurotransmitter.

Smartphones offer different kinds of features and aside from sending messages or calling your loved ones, you can download different apps to maximize your smartphone experience. Today, you can use smartphones to play games, watch videos, listen to music, check your social media accounts and many other things. With the profusion of new features, the opportunity is increased to spend increasing time on your cellphone, and to derive increasing pleasure from it.

Warning Signs of Cellphone Addiction

Many people own smartphones these days so does this mean that almost everyone are addicted to their mobile phones? The answer is no. There are some criteria to determine whether a person is a smartphone addict. Below are some of the warning signs of cellphone addiction:

- **Calloused thumbs:** Calluses on thumbs are signs of overuse due to texting. Aside from calloused thumbs, another sign of over-texting is cramps in the fingers.
- **Neck strain:** Constantly looking down on your mobile phone can cause serious neck strain. Children who grew up using their mobile phones all the time may suffer from deformed necks due to the incorrect positioning of the neck vertebrae or bones.
- **Speaking in acronyms:** Using acronyms like OMG, LOL, and FTW may be signs of cellphone overuse. Many people who use their cellphone and texting too much have tendencies to use acronyms even when talking in real life.
- **Being unaware of the surroundings:** Many smartphone addicts are oblivious to what is happening in their surroundings. They are engrossed with their mobile phones and do not notice what's in front of them or around them. This is the reason why many cellphone addicts get involved in accidents while on the streets.
- **The phone becomes inseparable:** Mobile phone addicts get so attached to their phones that they are almost inseparable. They consider their phones as part of their bodies and experience being separated from their phone as simply painful and intolerable. They can experience panic attacks especially if they lose their phones.
- **Inability to function properly:** People with serious texting problems often are unable to function at work or in school. They are preoccupied about using their phones at all times. Thus they tend to forget their other obligations and responsibilities.

- **Is defensive when confronted:** A cellphone addict is often defensive when confronted about his or her addiction problem.

Comorbidity

Considerable research remains to be done around cyber-relational addictions, with specific focus on social networking, texting, and email use. However, some trends are beginning to emerge. Like many behavioral addictions, problematic usage of social connection opportunities online is comorbid with other Internet and general behavioral addictions (Nathan, 2016). Attention deficit disorders are commonly associated with problematic Internet use, and likely apply to this category specifically as well. Other obsessive-compulsive related disorders are also likely to have high rates of comorbidity. One case study examined a fifteen-year-old girl with child-onset ADD, OCD, trichotillomania and excessive Facebook use. The case discussion highlights many of the vulnerabilities and socio-familial concerns that may contribute to the development of this Internet-based addiction (Nathan, 2016).

Cyber Sexual Addictions

History and Epidemiology

As the Internet has grown in size and accessibility, so has the potential to profit from it, and Internet pornography represents a large portion of the total market. It is difficult to determine the exact size of the industry because the businesses are largely privately owned, and there is some debate about what should be labeled as an "adult" service. However, estimates suggest that the online pornography industry is at least a $10 billion industry, and that pornography accounts for nearly 70% of the total pay-per-view content online. As a result of the increased availability of sexual content online, researchers and clinicians are reporting an increase in the number of clients seeking help for their cyber sexual addictions (Kimberly S. Young, 2011). Though the large majority (80%) of Internet users who view sexual content could be considered recreational users and do not report any consequences stemming from their online behavior, 20% of individuals may suffer personal, vocational, and/or legal consequences for their use. As early as 2003, for example, the American Academy of Matrimonial Attorneys reported that cyber porn was a significant factor in two-thirds of all divorces.

The compulsive engagement in cyber-sexual content, a sub-group of both sexual addictions and Internet addictions, involves a pattern of out of control online sex-related behaviors that have significant consequences for the individual (Carnes, 2001). Because of the ease of access, it might be difficult to find a sex addict today who has not been involved in some way with cyber-sexual content – some even suggest that the rise in prevalence of sexual addictions between 1980 and 1999 is due mainly to sexual content online. These cyber-sexual behaviors and content may consist of a number of activities, including persistent viewing of pornography, online affairs, or things like "sexting," and may occur on a number of platforms, including personal computers, laptops and mobile devices (Kimberly (Young, 2011). Patrick Carnes writes:

> In today's world it is possible to meet someone on a dating site or a hookup app, to flirt with that person via text and sext, to have virtual sex with that person via webcam, and then brag about this hot new relationship on social media – all without ever being in the same room with that person (or even the same country). (Carnes, 2001).

Furthermore, some research into Internet use shows that people communicate and behave differently online: a phenomenon called the *online disinhibition effect* (Kimberly S. Young, 2011). Accessing pornographic content online is easy, affordable and anonymous, a perilous mixture for those who may be pre-disposed to developing a sexual or Internet addiction. Sexual addictions are often highly secretive and pre-occupying; addicts may suffer socially as they distance themselves from their network of family and friends. The fear of being discovered may cause immense shame and anxiety, and addicts often struggle with the tension between their actions and their personal values and belief systems. Additionally, despite stereotypes of typical visitors to online pornography websites, many users are female, often from higher income brackets (Kimberly S. Young, 2011). An Internet watchdog group, Covenant Eyes, has found that 21% of young women (18-30 years of age) report accessing online pornography several times each week. This challenges the preconceived notion of who might be vulnerable to these kinds of addictions and should serve as a reminder to continue to examine cases individually, rather than based on stereotypes.

Clinical Presentation and Diagnostic Options

Clinicians may see a variety of clients who seek help for their cybersex addictions, or work with the families and partners of those who engage in such additions. In many ways, there is little distinction between sex addiction and cyber-sexual addiction, especially as most sex addicts utilize the Internet for some form of their sexual behaviors (Carnes, 2001). As such it may be useful to consider criteria for both Internet and sex addiction. As with many behavioral addiction concerns, one of the primary objectives for any clinician will be helping the client to find a boundary between excessive and recreational behavior, a level that may be clouded by the fact that sexual drives can vary between individuals and the fact that this behavior is a natural and appropriate drive. Though there are differences among various approaches to sexual addiction, these core features overlap and may be useful to help a clinician distinguish between normal and abnormal sexual behavior:

1. Excessive sexual behavior, generally outside the context of sustained relationships
2. Intense and persistent urges to perform such sexual behavior, similar to the drug craving found in chemical addictions
3. Continuation of sexual behavior despite the potential to cause significant harm with regard to personal, occupational and financial domains and/or physical health, and
4. Difficulty stopping the behavior despite repeated attempts or in the face of significant negative consequences (Ascher & Levounis, 2015).

The following criteria for Internet addiction may also be helpful for consideration:

1. Internet addicts as compared to other users demonstrate a loss of impulse control: despite consequences, addicts will continue use
2. Average online usage is excessive and basic tasks are interrupted (for example: sleep deprivation, and then resulting patterns of lateness to work or school)
3. Client has made several unsuccessful efforts to control, cut back or stop their use
4. The Internet serves as a way to regulate mood
5. The client stays online longer than intended and may lie to others about the extent of their use. (Kimberly S. Young, 2011)

In addition, signs of distress when use is reduced and a preoccupation with Internet usage may serve as important criteria for understanding an individual client's potential Internet addiction. Clinicians also have access to a number of assessments that have been modified to assess for cyber-sexual addictions; the Internet Sex Screening Test and a modified Sexual Addiction Screening Test may be particularly useful (Kimberly S. Young, 2011).

In both of the lists of criteria above, the fundamental difference between recreational access of online sexual content and cyber-sexual addictions is the impact on functioning. It is when these experiences are abused to the point where they become all-consuming and interfere with the individual's life despite their attempts to curb their use, that they cross into the category of addiction. Additionally, other symptoms may be seen in individuals with cybersex, and specifically, Internet porn addictions. A 2012 self-report survey of self-identified sex addicts suggested that almost 30% reported issues with sexual dysfunction (Carnes, 2001). This dysfunction is not only related to a physical need to recover from orgasm, but also to the variety of content available online that may reduce attraction to "real-life" partners (Rosenberg et al, 2014).

Much like gambling addictions, certain individuals may be more at risk to develop a cyber-sexual addition. Because sex serves a biological purpose and releases the neurochemical oxytocin, it has been suggested that oxytocin levels in sex addicts may be partially responsible for the dysfunctional behavior (Sun et al., 2012). Other clinicians believe that sexual dysfunction stems largely from attachment disorders, where individuals have difficulty forming stable bonds with others. Similarly, clients who have history of trauma can potentially manifest their traumatic past in a sexual addiction. Also, cognitive distortions play an important role in sexual addictions. Feelings of worthlessness, negative self-image, fear and distrust of others, among other distorted ways of thinking can lead individuals to the belief that sex will relieve their issues. This creates a cycle as guilt and negative feelings about self are a result of engaging in addiction-related behaviors. The person is distressed, seeks pleasure and soothing in the form of orgasm, and then experiences shame and distress at sexual behavior, perpetuating the cycle.

Comorbidity

Similar to gambling disorders, research around sexual addictions shows high rates of comorbidity. Because sexuality is intricately tied up with self-esteem and body image, sexual disorders have high comorbidity with eating disorders. Research has estimated that this could be as high as 38% (Carnes,

2001). Substance use is also commonly paired with sexual addictions. About 42% of sex addicts have co-occurring issues with substance use. Among cocaine abusers, estimates show that 50-70% also have issues with sexual compulsions. Additionally, affective disorders are common among sex addicts, and 72% report suicidal ideation. Other compulsive behaviors, such as gambling, shoplifting, compulsive shopping and other forms of behavioral addictions are also common. One study found that of a pool of sex addicts only around 10% reported just one addiction. Trauma also has significantly high rates of comorbidity with sexual addictions. Some research has shown that 97% of sex addicts were emotionally abused as children, 72% were physically abused, and as many as 81% were sexually abused (Sun et al., 2012).

Net Compulsions – Online Shopping, Online Gambling and other Online Addictions

History and Epidemiology

Some forms of Internet addiction fall most neatly under a broad category of "net compulsions," including online gambling, shopping, and problematic eBay use, among others. Like the offline version of these habits, there is potential for financial, occupational and relational issues as a result of excessive online engagement. The Internet, however, is a unique location for these activities because it provides unparalleled accessibility and privacy when engaging in these behaviors online. Cutting out trips to a casino or mall may allow addicts to continue use without detection.

Internet gambling is growing rapidly in popularity and represents a large shift in the culture of gambling over the past twenty years (Kimberly S. Young, 2011). Like with sexual addictions, experts predict that a shift to online gambling will increase prevalence rates of problematic gambling, changing the nature of gambling itself (making it less social, less regulated, more accessible and socially acceptable). Those who engage in gambling online are also more susceptible to developing problematic gambling habits than those who gamble in more traditional settings. One factor that increases vulnerability in online gambling is that electronic cash for many does not have the same psychological value as real cash, which allows gamblers to temporarily suspend their judgement about what might be an appropriate amount to spend. Also, it is typical that in practice or demo mode there is a heightened chance of winning, which distorts the perceptions around chances of winning, even in those who rationally understand their statistical odds. The demographic picture of online gamblers is typically a young, single well-educated male, typically in a professional/managerial role.

Compulsive online shopping is also a growing area of clinical concern. As online shopping has increase in popularity, vulnerable populations may suffer from targeted advertising and the excitement of near instant gratification – it is now difficult to shop online without being further inundated with images in other websites generated from your browsing history. It is estimated that between 5-8% of Americans suffer from a shopping addiction (Rosenberg & Feder, 2014). As with gambling, online shopping may change some of the features of this activity, as online shoppers are may be more likely to suffer social anxiety and they can use their online access to avoid social interaction. Also, as online stores are typically available around the clock, there may be more difficulty in preventing access and inhibition may be weakened by this continued potential. Typically, more women than men are seen for shopping addictions. A related issue is online auction houses, eBay in particular, where pathological users may experience both the rush of winning found in online gambling and the gratification of online shopping.

Clinical Presentation and Diagnostic Options

While the DSM-5 recognizes pathological gambling, there is no category for net compulsions per se. Simple modifications of the criteria for problematic gambling can be made for understanding online gambling, online shopping and other compulsive online behavior. The DSM-5 presents the following diagnostic criteria for pathological gambling disorder:

1. Needs to gamble with increasing amounts of money in order to achieve the desired excitement.
2. Is restless or irritable when attempting to cut down or stop gambling.
3. Has made repeated unsuccessful efforts to control, cut back, or stop gambling.
4. Is often preoccupied with gambling (e.g., having persistent thoughts of reliving past gambling experiences, handicapping or planning the next venture, thinking of ways to get money with which to gamble).
5. Often gambles when feeling distressed (e.g., helpless, guilty, anxious, depressed).
6. After losing money gambling, often returns another day to get even ("chasing" one's losses).
7. Lies to conceal the extent of involvement with gambling.

8. Has jeopardized or lost a significant relationship, job, or educational or career opportunity because of gambling.
9. Relies on others to provide money to relieve desperate financial situations caused by gambling (Association, 2013).

Of the above criteria, four (or more) of the nine listed are required for a diagnosis. Modifying the criteria above to diagnose online shopping addiction is as easy as changing "gambling" to "online shopping," however, these criteria are not formally recognized and as such should be used only as a way to understand an individual patient and not to confer a diagnosis.

Further understanding comes from alternative conceptualizations. Dr. Kimberly Young created the ACE Model – an acronym that helps explain compulsive online behaviors (Young, 2011). The **A** stands for Accessibility; the easy and immediate access to gambling, shopping or other behaviors online. The **C** stands for Control; the personal sense of control an individual has over their online activities. Because laptops and mobile devices are highly personalized and considered private, an addict can engage in a behavior without arousing much suspicion and can set up their device to enable continued use. The **E** stands for Excitement; the intense emotions felt when engaging in net compulsions, which in turn becomes a reinforcement for the behavior. This model may prove useful to clinicians who serve addicts and their families in helping to understand the behavior and its allure.

Certain individuals may be more at risk for developing these kinds of Internet addictions. Research results show that there may be a neurobiological and genetic risk factor for developing pathological gambling; impacted individuals may be pre-disposed to deficits in dopamine which puts them at high risk for pleasure-generating addictions (Sun et al., 2012). Another risk factor is history of trauma: a recent study showed that 64% of the individuals in treatment for gambling addiction had a history of abuse (Sun et al., 2012). Additional risk factors include age, male gender, social modeling, personality risk factors including impulsivity and sensation seeking traits, poorly developed coping skills, low self-esteem, and lack of social support. As with all addictions, no specific trait can be identified and the traits or client history listed above should be considered risk factors, not direct causation.

Signs and Symptoms of Online Gambling Addiction

Online gambling addiction has no physical signs and symptoms, unlike alcohol or drug addiction. However, here are the signs and symptoms to look out for.

- **Secretive about gambling activities:** An online gambling addict is secretive with his or her gambling habits and activities—or online activities as a whole. They become defensive when they are confronted about their online gambling activities.
- **Gambling even if they don't have money:** Online gambling addicts continue to gamble even if they don't have money to bet. As a result, they cannot pay their bills, let alone their debts. Further, they cannot perform their financial obligations to their families. Thus, they tend to borrow more money, sell their stuff or even steal to fund their online gambling habits.
- **Trouble controlling their gambling habits:** Once a person becomes addicted to online gambling, it is difficult for them to control their gambling habits despite what their friends and family tell them.

Why Is Online Gambling More Dangerous Than Conventional Gambling?

Online gambling, just like conventional gambling, may pose a considerable danger to those who are addicted to it. But why does it come with more dangers than conventional gambling? Below are the reasons why online gambling is considered to be more dangerous than conventional gambling.

- **Online gamblers are anonymous:** Conventional gamblers spend a lot of time in the casino, thus everyone notices. Online gamblers, on the other hand, can do their normal tasks without divulging that they are online addicts. They can remain in anonymity so their friends or family won't be aware that they are gambling.
- **Accessibility:** Part of the treatment for gambling addicts is to avoid the "act." This means that they can avoid casinos, bars or other locations where gambling might be possible. Online gambling, on the other hand, is much more difficult to treat because it is accessible online. It is virtually impossible not to use the Internet these days.
- **Online Banking:** Most online gambling addicts spend a lot of money to feed their addiction. Access to online banking makes it easier for online gambling addicts to spend more money in just a few clicks. Some online gambling sites provide electronic money to their players, but most gamblers forget that electronic money is still real money and they must pay using their credit cards if they lose the game.
- **Online gambling is legal yet not regulated:** In many places, online gambling particularly online casinos are legal but not regulated. So, anyone can enter online casino sites and bet. For instance, underage children can enter online gambling sites by faking their identities.

- **It is deceptive:** Online gambling is very deceptive as the online gambling website uses bots that are programmed to act like real human players to encourage the online gambler to raise his or her bets.
- **It can be linked with other types of addictions:** Online gambling provides convenience as well as comfort. And it puts online gamblers at risk of engaging in other types of addictions such as alcohol or drugs.
- **Identity theft:** Because most payments in online gambling sites are made through credit cards, there is a possibility of online gamblers being victimized by identity theft because of the personal information that they have provided to the website.
- **It is difficult to recover:** With the Internet making online gambling more accessible, it is more difficult for recovering addicts to avoid relapse.

Online Shopping Addiction

Online shopping addiction is an example of a net compulsion. People who are addicted to online shopping feel extremely happy once they do "retail therapy." Their brains release high amounts of dopamine and endorphins which are chemical signals that make people happy. Production of too much endorphins and dopamine can lead to feelings of addiction, especially when associated with a popular activity–in this case, shopping. Most online shopping addicts start out as traditional "shopaholics." The popularity of Internet shopping created a convenient extension for their addiction as they can now do uninhibited shopping right in the comforts of their own homes.

Online shopping addiction is more addictive than offline compulsive shopping, and more costly, too. Most online shoppers pay for their purchases using their credit cards and this often creates an illusion that they are not spending money. To make matters worse, auction websites such as eBay and Amazon make online shopping more accessible, attractive, and exhilarating for online shopaholics by organizing online bids where people can try to outbid each other and "win" merchandise.

What feeds online shopping addiction is not only the feeling of being "high" that you get after purchasing something online, but also the online forums and chatrooms where online shopaholics can interact to boost their confidence.

The rise of the Internet has made online gambling not only possible, but one of the biggest forms of Internet addiction. Today, there are thousands of Internet gambling websites that feed people's addiction. Online gambling websites are very accessible and this is the primary reason why many adolescents are addicted to online gambling, because there is no way to regulate the age of people that join these websites out of fun.[4] But what may start out as pure entertainment can become a stepping stone towards Internet addiction.

Why is online gambling so addictive? Perhaps the most important motivation for people to become addicted to online gambling is the strong desire to earn money. This is the top reason why different types of online gambling such as sports' betting and online casinos abound. Most young people have access to the Internet and the unrestricted access of online gambling websites has led to the rise of online gambling addiction, particularly in younger people.

Signs of An Online Shopping Addict

It is hard to distinguish an online shopping addict from someone who just loves shopping. Many people love to shop, but this does not mean that they are shopping addicts. Going on a shopping spree every once in a while is not considered as a shopping addiction. Below are some of the signs of an online addict.

- **They think too much about shopping:** Online shopaholics think too much about online shopping even when they are not currently engaged in such an activity. Thinking too much about online shopping can affect the daily activities of an online shopaholic.
- **They unknowingly spend too much money even on useless things:** Remember that online shopaholics do not shop because they need the items that they want to buy. Instead, they shop because they just want to feel the "happy feelings" experienced when purchasing items online. As a result, their excessive shopping behavior often leads them to overspend their money unknowingly on useless stuffs.
- **They lie about their online purchases:** Many online shopaholics lie about their online purchases and they might also become too defensive when people ask them about their online shopping habits.
- **They accumulate debt:** Because of their excessive shopping habits, most online shopaholics accumulate substantial debts. So, they end up neglecting their financial responsibilities to their families—or even their personal financial responsibilities.
- **Easily feel depressed:** Many online shopaholics have the tendency to become depressed especially if they cannot go online and shop. For them, nothing can elevate their moods other than shopping.

- **They bookmark online shops:** Online addicts like to keep updated on the latest looks from their favorite online shops. If a person has too many online websites bookmarked on their web browser, then it might be a sign that they are an online shopping addict.
- **Constantly checking out online retailers:** When a person cannot start their day without checking their favorite online shops as part of their daily routine. And since online promotions can change within hours, online shopping addicts may also check them regularly throughout the day.

Online shopping addiction has both short-term and long-term effects. The short-term effect of shopping addiction is the feeling of positivity. However, after the feeling of high is over, positive feelings are often mixed with guilt and anxiety.

The long-term effects of online shopping addiction include financial problems due to incurring substantial credit card debt. They can also damage personal relationships because of their inability to control their purchases.

Comorbidity

Net compulsions are associated with a number of comorbid concerns. A 2001 study of pathological gamblers found that 62% had comorbid mental health diagnoses (Ibanez et al, 2001). Commonly, there was overlapping diagnosis with personality disorders, substance use disorders, and other psychiatric concerns, including major depression and ADHD (Sun et al., 2012). Though there has been some research on causality, individual patients will likely have unique profiles of correlated issues that all may interact and therefore perpetuate one another. Compulsive shoppers often have co-occurring mood disorders, eating disorders, substance use disorders, other impulse-control or behavioral addiction concerns and personality disorders. Overall, net compulsions are associated with impulsivity and novelty seeking. A highly trained clinician should help to focus attention on the highest priority issues and to work to address underlying concerns.

References

Andreassen, C., Torsheim, T., Brunborg, G., & Pallesen, S. (2012). Development of a Facebook Addiction Scale. *Psychological Reports, 110*(2), 501-17.

Ascher, M. S., & Levounis, P. (2015). *The Behavioral Addictions* (First edition. ed.). Washington, DC: American Psychiatric Publishing, a division of American Psychiatric Association.

Association, A. P. (2013). Highlights of Changes From DSM-IV-TR to DSM-5. Retrieved from http://www.dsm5.org/Documents/changes from dsm-iv-tr to dsm-5.pdf

Burnell Kaitlyn and Kuther Tara L.. Cyberpsychology, Behavior, and Social Networking. October 2016, 19(10): 621-627. doi:10.1089/cyber.2016.0209.

Deb, A. (2015). Phantom vibration and phantom ringing among mobile phone users: A systematic review of literature. *Asia-Pacific Psychiatry, 7*(3), 231-239.

Carnes, P. (2001). *Out of the shadows: understanding sexual addiction* (3rd ed.). Center City, MN: Hazelden Information & Edu.

Kimberly S. Young, C. N. d. A. (Ed.) (2011). *Internet Addition: A Handbook and Guide to Evaluation and Treatment.* Hoboken, NJ: John Wiley & Sons Inc.

Nathan, Deepa, Shukla, Lekhansh, Kandasamy, Arun, & Benegal, Vivek. (2016). Facebook role play addiction--a comorbidity with multiple compulsive--impulsive spectrum disorders. *Journal of Behavioral Addictions, 5*(2), 373.

Petry, N.M., & Weinstock, J. (2007). Internet gambling is common in college students and associated with poor mental health. *The American Journal on Addictions, 16*, 325-330.

Pietrzak, R.H., & Petry, N.M. (2005). Antisocial personality disorder is associated with increased severity of gambling, medical, drug and psychiatric problems among treatment-seeking pathological gamblers. *Society for The Study of Addiction, 100*, 1183-1193.

Rosenberg, K. P., & Feder, L. C. (2014). *Behavioral addictions: criteria, evidence, and treatment.* London ; Waltham, MA: Academic Press.

Rosenberg, K., Carnes, P., & O'Connor, S. (2014). Evaluation and Treatment of Sex Addiction. *Journal of Sex & Marital Therapy, 40*(2), 77-91.

Sun, A.-P., Ashley, L. L., & Dickson, L. (2012). *Behavioral Addiction: Screening, Assessment, and Treatment.* Las Vegas, NV: Central Recovery Press.

O'Keeffe, Gwenn Schurgin, & Clarke-Pearson, Kathleen. (2011). The impact of social media on children, adolescents, and families. *Pediatrics, 127*(4), 800.

Chapter 6 Resources

This section gives a list of resources for those who wish to seek out more information on the topics presented in the chapter. Again, when considering the history and changes to the DSM surrounding behavioral addictions, please note that many resources were created prior to the release of the Complete reference appear above under References.

Printed Resources

The following books/chapters are selections that may help deepen your knowledge of this subject

Internet Addiction: A Handbook and Guide to Evaluation and Treatment, Young and Nabuco de Abreu

Behavioral Addictions: Criteria, Evidence, and Treatment, Rosenberg and Feder
Chapter 4: Problematic Online Gaming
Chapter 5: Internet Addiction Disorder: Overview and Controversies
Chapter 6: Social Networking Addiction: An Overview of Preliminary Findings

Behavioral Addiction, An-Pyng Sun, PhD
Chapter 7: Inherent Addiction

The Behavioral Addictions, Ascher and Levounis
Chapter 6: Internet Gaming Disorder: Virtual or Real?
Chapter 7: Internet Addiction: The Case of Henry, the "Reluctant Hermit"
Chapter 8: Texting and E-mail Problem Use

Online Resources

The Center for Internet and Technology Addiction
http://virtual-addiction.com/
The Psychology of Cyberspace
http://users.rider.edu/~suler/psycyber/

Addiction Recovery
http://www.addictionrecov.org/Addictions/index.aspx?AID=43

Journal Articles

Yau, Y. H. C., Crowley, M. J., Mayes, L. C., & Potenza, M. N. (2012). Are Internet use and video-game-playing addictive behaviors? Biological, clinical and public health implications for youths and adults. *Minerva Psichiatrica,53*(3), 153–170.

ROBERTS, J. A., PETNJI YAYA, L. H., & MANOLIS, C. (2014). The invisible addiction: Cell-phone activities and addiction among male and female college students. *Journal of Behavioral Addictions*, 3(4), 254–265. http://doi.org/10.1556/JBA.3.2014.015

Kim, Y., Jeong, J.-E., Cho, H., Jung, D.-J., Kwak, M., Rho, M. J., … Choi, I. Y. (2016). Personality Factors Predicting Smartphone Addiction Predisposition: Behavioral Inhibition and Activation Systems, Impulsivity, and Self-Control. PLoS ONE, 11(8), e0159788. http://doi.org/10.1371/journal.pone.0159788

M. D. Griffiths 2000 Does Internet and computer "addiction" exist? Some case study evidence. *CyberPsychology & Behavior* 3 2 211 218. CrossRef

O'Keeffe, Gwenn Schurgin, & Clarke-Pearson, Kathleen. (2011). The impact of social media on children, adolescents, and families. *Pediatrics, 127*(4), 800. Ito, Mizuko, & Itåo, Mizuko. (2009). *Living and learning with new media: Summary of findings from the digital youth project* (The John D. and Catherine T. MacArthur Foundation reports on digital media and learning Living and learning with new media).

Boyd, Danah. (2007) "Why Youth (Heart) Social Network Sites: The Role of Networked Publics in Teenage Social Life." MacArthur Foundation Series on Digital Learning – *Youth, Identity, and Digital Media Volume* (ed. David Buckingham). Cambridge, MA: MIT Press.

Hansen, S., Crandall, Heather M., & Caputo, John S. (2012). *The Facebook Effect: Considering the Influence of Facebook on the User's Sense of Community,*ProQuest Dissertations and Theses.

Griffiths, M. (2012). Internet sex addiction: A review of empirical research. *Addiction Research & Theory, 2012, Vol.20(2), P.111-124,* 20(2), 111-124.

Laier, C., Schulte, F., & Brand, M. (2013). Pornographic Picture Processing Interferes with Working Memory Performance. *Journal of Sex Research, 50*(7), 642-652.

Wegmann, Elisa, Stodt, Benjamin, & Brand, Matthias. (2015). Addictive use of social networking sites can be explained by the interaction of Internet use expectancies, Internet literacy, and psychopathological symptoms. *Journal of Behavioral Addictions, 4*(3), 155.

Andreassen, C., Torsheim, T., Brunborg, G., & Pallesen, S. (2012). Development of a Facebook Addiction Scale. *Psychological Reports, 110*(2), 501-517.

Griffiths, M. (2012). Facebook Addiction: Concerns, Criticism, and Recommendations–A Response to Andreassen and Colleagues. *Psychological Reports, 110*(2), 518-520.

Kuss, D. J., Griffiths, M. D., & Binder, J. F. (2013). Internet addiction in students: Prevalence and risk factors. *Computers in Human Behavior, 29*(3), 959-966.

Billingsley, Stephanie. (2014). Sex addiction treatment: Overcoming stigma. *Addiction Professional, 12*(6), 38.

Goodmon, Leilani B., Smith, Patrick L., Ivancevich, Danica, & Lundberg, Sofie. (2014). Actions speak louder than personality: Effects of Facebook content on personality perceptions. *North American Journal of Psychology, 16*(1), 105.

Online Videos

Quitting Social Media
https://www.youtube.com/watch?v=3E7hkPZ-HTk

What You Need to Know about Internet Addiction, Dr. Kimberly Young
https://www.youtube.com/watch?v=vOSYmLER664

Hooked, Hacked, Hijacked
https://www.youtube.com/watch?v=aqhzFd4NUPI

CHAPTER 7

Intervention and Treatment for Internet Addictions

Chapter Overview

This chapter will discuss intervention and treatment for Internet addictions. First, we will present case studies for the various categories of Internet disorders. Then we will give an overview of the types of therapies used in the treatment of behavioral addictions. Additionally, this chapter will look at differences and similarities between harm-reduction based models of treatment and abstinence-only models of treatment.

Case Studies

The case studies presented below are offered as a way to begin understanding Internet addictions in the real world. In each case, consider the following questions:

1. How has this behavior crossed into clinically significant territory?
2. What concerns would I have if I were treating this individual?

3. What would I do first if I were treating this individual?
4. What issues may be underlying or comorbid?
5. How do I conceptualize this behavior on a broad scale within this particular client's life?

Social Media Addiction: Samantha is Social

Samantha is a 21-year-old Caucasian college student. Intake assessment reveals that her parents have been unable to support her through college and that during the summer she runs a fairly successful wedding photography business that helps her pay her tuition. Her clients find her typically from a social media app called Instagram. In previous years, she did not continue photography during the school year, but this year she is finding it hard to stay off Instagram. Samantha reports feeling successful and important when her photos reach a certain number of "likes" and that her former goal of becoming a veterinarian is no longer important to her. She admits that she is constantly on her phone during class, checking to see if there have been any new comments on her page, and that her grades are considerably worse than previous semesters. She is at risk of losing her academic scholarship if her grades do not improve. When asked about other issues she is experiencing in her life she shares that her boyfriend of two years recently broke up with her, citing that he said she cared more about her phone than she did about him.

Online Gaming Addiction: Jorge's Call to Duty

Jorge is a 20-year-old college student. Clinical interviews reveals that he is a successful student and, while his achievements should bring him a sense of accomplishment, he that he is depressed all the time and embarrassed that he is still a virgin. Though his academic performance is strong, his social skills are under-developed. Since moving away from home, Jorge has become increasingly consumed by an online game called Call of Duty, where he says he has made the best friends of his life. But he admits that he has spent the time he should have spent in class sleeping at home instead because his late night gaming sessions often go through the night. When asked, Jorge is able to identify other aspects of his life that are suffering as well – he has weight because he does not want to interrupt his gaming to eat, and his facial acne, once under good control, has come back due to his poor hygiene and eating habits.

Online Shopping Addiction: Sally's Secret Shopping

Sally is a 31-year-old female who has sought treatment because of her social anxiety. Further interview reveals that though she and her husband both make good money in their careers, they are struggling to make their mortgage payments because of the amount of items she purchases online. Most of the purchases she justifies by talking about the money she is saving by buying online rather than in a store and she states that she prefers to shop online because she doesn't have to deal with snobby salespeople. Sally's husband, who has attended the appointment with her, says he had no idea that her spending was so out of control because he does not have shared access to her accounts and she had previously been in charge of managing their combined finances. He also expresses frustration about her increasing isolation and how it has impacted their combined social lives.

Online Gambling Addiction: Richard's Roulette

Richard, a 65-year-old retired man, lives in a rural area of South Dakota where there is not much by way of entertainment except a large casino. Previously, he had regularly visited the casino for mostly social purposes, but since getting a laptop as a Christmas gift and discovering that he can access slots online, he has begun to spend less time with friends and is now spending hours online each day. He has sought therapy because he believes he has depression. Further questioning reveals that Richard's wife died suddenly, shortly before Christmas and he is still struggling with the loss of his partner.

Cyber-Sex Addiction: Laura's Online Lust

Laura is a 27-year-old woman who works as a manager of an advertising office of a large national company. She has sought out therapy due to a pattern of infidelity that has led to the end of several relationships over the last few years. She articulates feeling helpless to stop cheating on her partners because there is constant access and the online nature of many of these relationships allows her to hide the infidelity for some time before being discovered. Laura has had previous therapy to help her process some sexually traumatic experiences in her childhood, particularly the physical and sexual abuse she endured from a female nanny between the ages of five and eight.

General Internet Addiction: Nancy- Online All the Time

Nancy is a 25-year-old female graduate student currently enrolled in a Ph.D. program at a local university. She is reluctant to be in therapy, but was encouraged to go by her advisor, who has noted a decline in the quality of work and her focus level in the class she takes with him. When asked about her typical daily activities, Nancy lists all the TV shows she typically watches on Netflix and talks about how she will keep Netflix running almost all day long, using a second computer to read comics online. She is not concerned about how much time she spends online and says that she typically reads really interesting articles and constantly is learning new things. You note that Nancy seems tired and disheveled.

Internet Addiction or Lifestyle Preference – Where is the Line?

The concept of Internet Addiction had an ironic start – in 1995, Dr. Irving Goldberg, a moderator of an online chatroom for psychologists and psychiatrists, decided to modify DSM criteria from pathological gambling and jokingly spoofed these criteria to conjure up something he dubbed Internet Addiction Disorder (I.A.D). Much to his surprise, he received hundreds of responses from self-described addicts for a disorder he didn't believe in at all – he is quoted as having said that having a support group for Internet addicts "makes as much sense as having a support group for coughers". Despite the controversial beginning of this category of concerns, since 1998, literally billions of users have connected to the Internet, and online access has changed the way we conduct business, build relationships and even how we learn. For some, this dramatic shift in how we live is enough of a cause for concern.

Though society has dedicated considerable attention to substance use disorders, behavioral addictions in contrast are strikingly under-researched, even though prevalence rates are known to be high in the general population. Substances, of course, have immediate physical implications, whereas Internet addictions may begin in part because of their lack of observable symptoms. The physical implications of substance use (impairment) also have public health concerns such as drunk driving which brings them to public awareness. The illegal nature of many substances might also influence awareness around those concerns, though cyber-sexual addictions have in some part received attention because of the potential for inappropriate and even illegal content.

Harm Reduction or Abstinence Only

Treatment models for Internet addictions can vary between abstinence-based models or harm-reduction models (Rosenberg & Feder, 2014). Though this is an ongoing debate in the world of addiction treatment, with Internet addictions it is particularly complex. Unlike substance addictions, where a client could completely stop using the substance – for example, being "sober" and not drinking – in many Internet addictions the behavior in question may not be able to be completely avoided and instead must be managed controlled, instead. Abstinence based models may work well with certain cyber behaviors, where firewall software can block access to certain kinds of websites that are not necessary for daily use or for certain online games, or where software and accounts can be removed from personal computers. In this case, just like an alcoholic may need to avoid driving by a familiar bar on the way home from work each day, a pornography addict may need to block pornography websites from his or her computer.

In these cases, an abstinence model may work. The abstinence model is used by most 12-Step Programs which focus on the patient avoiding the behavior or substance altogether. However, a weakness of this model is that it is more difficult to achieve, especially with less cooperative patients, and it may be practically difficult for many Internet addictions because it may be impracticable to avoid email, discontinue the use of a cell phone, or avoid the Internet altogether. In these cases, a harm reduction approach may be the only viable option to pursue.

Harm reduction is often presented as a riskier option than abstinence only models because patients may be tempted to relapse to previous levels of use more frequently. Nonetheless, it may be a necessary alternative for some patients and some presenting concerns (Rosenberg & Feder, 2014). Overall, the harm reduction model tends to focus on progress and patient control rather than complete avoidance, and tends to fit better with Internet addictions. An addict to social media websites may not want to completely remove access because that would sever ties with valuable friendship and support networks, but may instead need to limit use to a certain number of hours per day or even restrict use to the weekends. Likewise, some patients want to reduce their online pornography habits rather than to abstain from them altogether, and each clinician must negotiate with his or her patients a preferred treatment model to pursue.

The Etiology of Internet Addictions – A Brief Look at the Psychology of the Web

Dr. Kimberly Young argues that the Internet is a particularly productive place for generating addictions (Kimberly S. Young, 2011). Here is a list of the especially seductive and addictive features of this medium.

1. *Accessibility* – Access to the Internet is now widespread and commonplace. With this reliable access, previous barriers for engagement in certain behaviors are removed. For example, an individual may have a computer at their desk at work. While carrying on social conversations during work hours may once have been regarded as inappropriate, individuals can now continue to instant message throughout the work day without fearing detection or the social disapproval of their colleagues.

2. *Affordability* – The Internet is becoming less expensive and certain things are available at reduced cost online. This may prove particularly tempting for those who struggle with online shopping addictions, as part of the thrill might be finding a deal on the desired item.

3. *Anonymity* – The privacy of the Internet allows people to engage in previously stigmatized activities without judgement and may increase feelings of comfort. Social anxieties are also reduced when engaging in behaviors online.

4. *Convenience* – The Internet is designed to be a convenient and user-friendly medium; many websites generate revenue based on traffic, which requires them to keep users interested and engaged in their content. Therefore, it is no surprise that vulnerable individuals find themselves hooked on certain online behaviors – that is precisely the intent of the designer.

5. *Escape* – The Internet may provide an avenue to escape from other emotional experiences or responsibilities. Some Internet activities may provide a numbing impact – such as hours of Netflix binging. Others might provide a "high," such the orgasm experienced in online pornography.

6. *Immersion and Dissociation* – Those who engage in the Internet may feel as though they have lost track of time or that they were in a trancelike state because of the deep immersion in the online environment. Some may even feel that they are able to be someone else online. This is attractive in ways similar to the feelings of escape as it may serve a mood modifying purpose.

7. *Disinhibition* – Internet users tend to open up more quickly in online mediums – a phenomenon referred to as hyper-personal communication. Users may also share opinions more strongly than in places mediated by social norms; this is easy to observe when reading the comments section of a YouTube video.

8. *Event Frequency* – Online content is designed to hook users, which often means that there is a significant amount of material available at one time. For example, multiple pornographic images on one screen, or rapid sequences of gambling events. This frequency is highly reinforcing.

9. *Interactivity* – The interactive nature of the Internet creates a positive feedback loop for users and may create an illusion of control. When placed in the context of problematic gambling, it is easy to see how the interactive nature may prove pleasurable for the user.

10. *Associability* – Online versions of activities often have the tendency to reduce the social content of these activities – for example, online shopping is done alone, whereas a shopping trip to the mall involves interaction with a number of people. Though some individuals find a social outlet in the Internet (through cyber-relational networks) these relationships are different than in-person connections and may not prove as fulfilling. (Kimberly S. Young, 2011)

Common Psychotherapeutic Interventions

Because of the lack of clarity of diagnostic criteria and assessment instruments for assessing Internet addictions, there are few treatments that have gained evidence-based status for treating these concerns (Ascher & Levounis, 2015). Treatments are typically offered on a case-by-case basis. Many substance use treatment models can be adapted for use with addicted patients and their families (Rosenberg & Feder, 2014). In this section we will briefly discuss some of the theories of treatment, options for group therapy, and family therapy. Overall, emerging research in this field will help clinicians tailor their treatment to specific client concerns. Though some specifics are discussed here, clinicians should be aware that there are significant limitations in treatment knowledge for Internet addictions. Many studies have relatively small sample sizes and may involve non-representative samples. Moreover, outcomes vary across studies in part because what constitutes a positive outcome for a client with an Internet addiction in itself may vary from person to person. Also, high rates of comorbid mental health concerns complicate the treatment picture for many individuals with Internet addictions. Though this may sound bleak, increasing clinical awareness is an important step – clients who are asked about their Internet behaviors have a higher likelihood of receiving treatment for these issues.

Behavioral Management for Internet Addictions

Some elements of Internet addictions might be best managed by behavioral interventions (Kimberly S. Young, 2011). This includes managing computer use and broader environmental management. For example, for a patient with a known cyber-sexual addiction, restricting their personal computer access to high traffic, public areas may prevent extended access to websites with sexual content. Screensavers that have photos of important people may also help remind people about their commitment to their goals to avoid certain behaviors. Electronic management may also be a useful way for dealing with various forms of Internet-based addictions. This might involve using filters or services that can block certain content. Monitoring software might also prove useful; these services track computer usage and report viewed content to a third party.

Providing patients with useful "dashboards," assessments, or tools can be useful elements to support behavioral management. One example of such a tool appears below. This list could be given to clients as a handout to assist them with monitoring and intervening in relation to their Internet behavior:

Set goals when using the Internet: Set a schedule on when you are going to use the Internet during the day. This prevents you from browsing online all the time. You can also reward yourself for using the Internet within your set amount of time and especially when you have completed an important online task or chore.

- **Go offline on certain times of the day:** Make it a habit to unplug from the Internet at certain times of the day especially when you are doing something important like driving, having dinner with family, or if you are in an important meeting.
- **Do not bring your gadgets to bed:** Gadgets emit blue light that can disrupt your sleep. But, more importantly, taking your gadgets to bed only feeds your compulsion to use the Internet for whatever purpose you might have. So, the next time you are preparing for a shut eye, turn off your gadgets and leave them somewhere in the bedroom where you cannot easily reach for them.

- **Replace your Internet compulsion with other activities:** Most people get into the habit of using the Internet excessively when they get lonely or bored. So, if you are lonely and you have the urge to do online shopping or gambling, then devise ways on how you can fill idle time without using the Internet. Examples of things that you can do to take your mind off the Internet is by reading a book, meditating or engaging in hobbies that you enjoy.

- **Engage in interactive activities with other Internet addicts:** If your friends are also Internet addicts then it is difficult to curb your habit if you are surrounded with like-minded individuals. If you find yourself in this situation, play a "phone stack" game if you are out to have lunch with your friends. Set your gadgets face down on the table and no one can check his or her device throughout the game. The one who cannot resist picking up their phone must pay everyone's check.

- **Remove apps from your gadgets:** Remove apps on your computer, tablet, or smart phone that are related to social networking and others that feed on your addiction. Having these apps on your gadgets feed your compulsion to constantly check for updates.

- **Limit your Internet use:** Most people who are addicted to the Internet are struggling with the fear of missing out. This can be very aggravating to people suffering from Internet addiction. By limiting your Internet use, you must accept that you are likely to miss certain unimportant things like gossip, breaking news, and updates from other people. But look on the bright side, missing out on these things and not being reliant on technology can be liberating.

- **Identify external stoppers:** Use things that prompt you to log off from the Internet. This is to help you develop a natural alarm so that you can voluntarily log off from the Internet. To train yourself, set an alarm and log off once it goes off. Do this on a regular time to develop it into a habit.

- **Abstain from the Internet on a specific time or day:** Abstinence from the Internet is also another great way to curb Internet addiction. However, this does not mean that you can no longer engage in using other applications. You only abstain on things or aspects that you are addicted to. For instance, if you are addicted to online shopping or gambling, abstain from visiting shopping or gambling websites on a particular day. If you can, test your tolerance by increasing your days of abstinence by adding more day at a time.[6]

- **Use reminder cards:** There are times when not logging on to the Internet can be very overwhelming. If this happens, you might succumb to your weakness and try using the Internet again. What you can do is to use reminder cards to keep yourself on the right track and focus on your goals. To help you further, make sure that you include in your reminder card the benefits of cutting down your Internet use.

- **Make a personal inventory:** Whether you are trying to cut down your Internet use or abstaining from a particular online application or website, it is important to take a personal inventory on what you need to cut out from your life. Moreover, list activities that you are doing less because of your excessive Internet use. When you make the inventory, rank the importance of the activities that you have on your list based on how these activities have improved the quality of your life. This strategy will help you become more aware of the different choices that you have when it comes to using the Internet.

Motivational Interviewing

Motivational interviewing is often helpful in the early stages of addiction treatment, where high levels of ambivalence are common (Rosenberg & Feder, 2014). This therapeutic technique is a collaborative conversation style that works to strengthen an individual's motivation and commitment to change by exploring the positive impacts and negative consequences of a given behavior. Often, individuals struggling with addiction will have conflicting desires: both wanting to continue their behavior but also wanting to avoid the consequences. Motivational interviewing can help patients clarify their struggles. When utilized skillfully, motivational interviewing can help patients moderate or change behaviors they have previously found difficult to stop themselves, and can also empower clients to make these decisions on their own volition (Miller and Rose, 2009). Ambivalence is not seen as resistance, nor are patients asked to accept that they are at rock bottom. Research on motivational interviewing shows that it can be used successfully to address a number of concerns including obesity, addictions, depression, HIV safety/awareness, among others.

Cognitive Behavioral Therapy (CBT)

Cognitive behavioral therapy is a the most-researched treatment option for Internet addictions (Rosenberg & Feder, 2014). This short-term, goal-oriented treatment involves a therapist and patient discussing the maladaptive thoughts of a patient with the goal of then changing behaviors and emotions. During early stages of treatment, the clinician focuses on the behavioral aspects of the addiction and the situations that trigger the addictive behavior. As the treatment progresses, the focus is on the cognitive aspects that have developed. For example, CBT addresses the cognitions that serve as triggers that cause the excessive Internet use. Internet addicts suffer from distorted views about themselves and the world, and this method is aimed at restructuring the cognitive processes by allowing individuals to re-script their negative thoughts. With the method, patients can understand the reason why they are using the Internet problematically, and modify their thinking to address the feelings that compel its use. Once the individual is aware of the patterns of their faulty thinking and reasoning, they can challenge their thoughts and therefor break the cycle of addictive behavior.

CBT has been shown to have positive impact in treating a wide-group of issues including anxiety, depression and addictions. In relation to Internet addictions, CBT can be used to discuss the maladaptive thoughts related to addictive behaviors and create strategies to compete with these maladaptive patterns (Rosenberg & Feder, 2014). Patients may work to identify patterns of abuse, avoid or better manage high-risk situations, and cultivate engagement in more positive substitute behaviors (Herkov, 2016). Because this style of therapy is goal directed and requires active participation, clients are often asked to complete homework assignments as part of their treatment process.

Dialectical Behavioral Therapy (DBT)

Dialectical behavioral therapy (DBT), created by Marsha Linnehan, also may be used as an intervention with Internet addiction clients. Originally created to address chronically suicidal Borderline Personality Disorder clients, DBT can be modified for use in conjunction with CBT modalities (PsychCentral, 2016) to treat Internet addictions. DBT has four main modules and clients learn skills to help manage their lives in each of the modules:

1. *Distress Tolerance.* Learning to "sit" with powerful urges and negative feelings- to experience them, to accept them, and to allow them to subside without using them as an automatic trigger to engage reflexively in the addictive behavior as a means of relief or satisfaction.
2. *Emotion Regulation.* Learn to control emotions through relaxation exercises and/or cognitive coping mechanisms, such as self-instruction.
3. *Mindfulness.* Cultivate an attunement, curiosity and acceptance of thoughts and feelings. Mindfulness is being open to, and curious about, experience, rather than evaluative, judgmental, or critical.
4. *Interpersonal Effectiveness.* Learn social skills that will enhance personal relationships and emotional intimacy and connection.

In a 2004 study on DBT with modifications for substance use researchers found that DBT reduced alcohol related symptoms by 1/3 and may also prove useful in treating associated issues including impulsivity (Dimeff, 2008). Further research is needed to determine the efficacy of this treatment for behaviorally addicted clients.

Psychodynamic Psychotherapy

Psychodynamic psychotherapy models may also prove useful in treating Internet addictions, particularly when done with a relational/interpersonal orientation. This therapeutic model addresses a patients affect regulation issues and discusses addiction as a failed solution for negotiating conflict around connecting with others (Rosenberg & Feder, 2014), often as it has arisen in early caregiving relationships. This intervention may challenge a patient to develop a full understanding of how addiction has been used as a mechanism to address or escape the challenges or pain of certain relationships and interpersonal experiences. Clinicians and clients work together to understand the underlying meaning of the addictive behaviors and ultimately to learn to develop more adaptive strategies and coping skills.

Group Therapy and Modified 12-Step Groups

Twelve-Step programs such as Alcoholics Anonymous, created by Dr. Bob Smith and Bill Wilson in 1935, are nearly synonymous with addiction recovery in popular culture (Lancer, 2016). This format has been adapted for a number of behavioral addictions with groups including: Gambler's Anonymous, Sex Addict's Anonymous, Overeaters Anonymous, Recovering Couples Anonymous (for recovering sex addicts) and Debtors Anonymous (for shopping addicts) (Ascher & Levounis, 2015; Rosenberg & Feder, 2014). Many of these programs focus on both in-person and online behaviors and their consequences.

The premise of the 12-step program is for the patient to use the following principles to deal with their addiction, often reviewed and applied during weekly group meetings with others recovering from behavioral addictions. Below are the twelve steps to treat Internet addiction.[7]

1. **Honesty:** Admit that you are powerless to overcome your addiction and your life has turned unmanageable because of it.
2. **Hope:** Believe that there is power greater than us that can restore your health back to you.

3. **Trust:** Trust your life over to someone who has more power of your condition.
4. **Truth:** Create a written moral inventory of yourself and be truthful about the things that you write about yourself.
5. **Integrity:** Admit to yourself and to others the nature of your wrong doings.
6. **Change of heart:** Embrace the fact that your higher power can remove your flaws and defects.
7. **Humility:** Ask your higher power with humility to remove your defects and shortcomings.
8. **Brotherly love:** Write a list of all people whom you have harmed due to your shortcomings and be willing to make amends with them.
9. **Reconciliation:** Reconcile directly to everyone whom you have harmed.
10. **Accountability:** Constantly create a personal inventory and admit immediately for every wrongdoing you have committed.
11. **Perseverance:** Persevere in admitting you're wrong. Never falter.
12. **Service and spirituality:** Having a spiritual awakening is the last step of the 12-step program and it is the stage when results and improvement are evident. To finalize the treatment, share the message with other people who are also suffering from the same condition as you do

Family Therapy

Internet addiction is oftentimes a family problem. And, like other mental health concerns, Internet addictions impact the whole family and not just the individual him or herself. In some cases, family members may be the first to seek treatment because of the negative impacts their loved one's addiction has on their lives. Internet addictions impact family member's health, trust, finances, and may even have social and/or legal repercussions (Grant, 2008).

Family therapy often focuses on several main areas which include (1) reducing the blame of Internet addicts for their compulsive behavior, (2) educating the family members on how addictive the Internet can be for everyone, (3) encouraging the family to assist with the recovery of their loved ones by taking new hobbies, and (4) improving the communication among family members so that the Internet addict will not seek fulfillment of their emotional needs online. The purpose of family therapy in treating Internet addiction is to create a strong sense of family support to enable patients to recover.

Broader family therapy can be similar to other group therapy work, but with the family (and often, friends) of the patient. Some 12-step programs involve families in special meetings that help educate them regarding how best to support their loved one. These models can help engage family members in identifying triggers and understanding the cycle of addiction. A useful discussion of how family members can respond to various situations commonly associated with behavioral addictions can be found in Grant's (2008), *Impulse Control Disorders.*

Mindfulness Based Techniques

Mindfulness-based treatments derive from Buddhist contemplative practice 2500 years ago and have been increasingly integrated into addiction treatment as a means of addressing the powerful feelings and urges that impel addictive behavior (Chen et al, 2014). A small but growing number of clinical trials have shown the effectiveness of mindfulness-based interventions, which in addiction therapy, are directed towards reducing cravings or the urge to engage in the addictive cycle (Rosenberg & Feder, 2014). As noted above, mindfulness is also integrated into a number of contemporary psychotherapy models such as DBT. Mindfulness, in addiction treatment, is meant to help shift the client's relationship with discomfort and help promote a non-judgmental stance with themselves and their thoughts. Rather than negative emotions leading habitually to drug use or engagement in an addictive behavior, mindfulness may allow the individual to be more aware of their own thoughts and emotions and interrupt the cycle.

Mindfulness Based Relapse Prevention (MBRP)

Mindfulness Based Relapse Prevention (MBRP) is a psychoeducational, 8-week, group based intervention that has gained some recent public attention after a 2014 study showed that compared to individuals in traditional 12-step relapse prevention programs, those in MBRP programs for substance use and heavy drinking experienced a significantly lower risk of relapse (Bowen et al, 2014). At a 12-month follow up, study participants who had received the MBRP intervention reported 1/3 less drug use days and a significantly higher probability of not engaging in any heavy drinking as compared to those who had received more typical treatments. The primary goals of MBRP are:

1. Develop awareness of personal triggers and habitual reactions, and learn ways to create a pause in this seemingly automatic process.

2. Change our relationship to discomfort, learning to recognize challenging emotional and physical experiences and responding to them in skillful ways.
3. Foster a nonjudgmental, compassionate approach toward ourselves and our experiences.
4. Build a lifestyle that supports both mindfulness practice and recovery. (Bowen et al, 2014).

Overall, mindfulness techniques can potentially help clinicians looking to support clients in building their own awareness.

Meditation, Breathing, Self-Control, Situation Awareness

Yoga is a spiritual practice that developed in India more than 5,000 years ago. It aims to help individuals to unite with their core through a series of physical stretches, posture and regulation of breath (Rosenberg & Feder, 2014). Yoga has developed a number of different kinds of practice including transcendental meditation and Sudarshan Kriya yoga. Transcendental meditation is a mantra based technique that strives or a state of alertness with no object of thought or perception (Rosenberg & Feder, 2014). Research on this meditation technique suggests that it may be useful in reducing negative outcomes and increasing self-concept and internal locus of control. Sudarshan Kriya yoga (SKY) is a breathing technique taught by thousands of trained teachers around the world that involves a complex set of breathing exercises. A randomized study done in 2006 compared recovering alcoholics who were taught SKY versus a control group. The experimental group had significant improvements on their scores on the Addiction Severity Index and reported improvements in quality of life. Though there are no direct studies for these alternative interventions with Internet addictions specifically, findings related to substance addictions can be used to understand how they might apply to Internet addictions. Further research is needed to determine which specific populations may benefit most from these alternative treatments.

Art Therapy

Because shame and privacy are key components of behavioral addictions, patients may need help sharing their experiences outside of the traditional psychotherapy set up (Sun, Ashley, & Dickson, 2012). Practitioners may consider incorporating creative therapy practices such as art, music, dance and drama into their treatment. These creative practices have been show to allow patients to explore thoughts and feelings in a safe way and allow for exploration of emotions typically associated with their out of control behaviors. For cyber-sexual addictions this technique may be particularly relevant as social norms surrounding discussion of sexual acts may make it difficult for clients to share their experiences. Overall, creative techniques have been shown to break down client defenses more quickly with less trauma. These methods could be particularly useful for helping addicted clients express themselves!

Psychopharmaceutical Treatments

Though no specific medications are recommended in the treatment of behavioral addictions, some practitioners recommend the use of psychiatric medications to help treat these concerns (Grant, 2008; Rosenberg & Feder, 2014; Sun et al., 2012). Medication is often prescribed to treat comorbid conditions, and many are proposing the use of anti-addiction medications such as N-acetylcysteine (NAC), a glutamate modulating agent that has also been found helpful in trials with substance use disorders to directly treat behavioral addictions. Another promising medication for the treatment of behavioral addictions are the opiate antagonists that presumably act by interfering with reward center pathways. Though provisional research is promising around these particular pharmacological treatments, patients with behavioral addictions are currently treated with traditional antidepressants, anti-compulsive medications, mood stabilizers, anxiolytics, and attention deficit medications. These medications are designed to address specific symptoms the person is experiencing, and not the Internet addiction itself. No specific medications are approved for the treatment of Internet addictions at this time.

Gambling disorder is one of the best-researched behavioral addictions and as such has produced the greatest volume of pharmacotherapy research studies (Sun et al., 2012). These studies suggest that certain medications may have a beneficial impact when treating gambling addictions. A double-blind study done in 2001 showed that naltrexone (an opiate antagonist) demonstrated superiority to placebo medications in subjects with pathological gambling. However, more than 20% of the study participants developed abnormal liver function tests during the 12-week long study (Grant, 2008). In another study on N-acetylcysteine, a glutamatergic agent, researchers found that it significantly reduced symptoms of pathological gambling in nearly 60% of the patients (Grant, 2008). Overall, these results support the potential value of additional research into medical treatments for behavioral addictions, particular those that show long term efficacy.

References

American Psychiatric Association. (2000). *Diagnostic and statistical manual of mental disorders* (4th ed., text rev.). doi:10.1176/appi.books.9780890423349.

Ascher, M. S., Levounis, P., & American Psychiatric Association. (2015). *The Behavioral Addictions* (First edition. ed.). Washington, DC: American Psychiatric Publishing, a division of American Psychiatric Association.

Association, A. P. (2013a). Highlights of Changes From DSM-IV-TR to DSM-5. Retrieved from http://www.dsm5.org/Documents/changes from dsm-iv-tr to dsm-5.pdf

Bowen, S., Chawla, N., Collins, S. E., Witkiewitz, K., Hsu, S., Grow, J., … Marlatt, A. (2009). Mindfulness-Based Relapse Prevention for Substance Use Disorders: A Pilot Efficacy Trial. *Substance Abuse, 30*(4), 295–305. http://doi.org/10.1080/08897070903250084

Chen, P., Jindani, F., Perry, J., & Turner, N. L. (2014). Mindfulness and problem gambling treatment. *Asian Journal of Gambling Issues and Public Health, 4*(1), 1.

Dimeff, L. A., & Linehan, M. M. (2008). Dialectical Behavior Therapy for Substance Abusers. *Addiction Science & Clinical Practice, 4*(2), 39–47.

Grant, J. E. (2008). *Impulse control disorders: a clinician's guide to understanding and treating behavioral addictions* (1st ed.). New York: W.W. Norton.

Rosenberg, K. P., & Feder, L. C. (2014). *Behavioral addictions: criteria, evidence, and treatment.* London ; Waltham, MA: Academic Press.

Kimberly S. Young, C. N. d. A. (Ed.) (2011). *Internet Addition: A Handbook and Guide to Evaluation and Treatment.* Hoboken, NJ: John Wiley & Sons Inc.

Lancer, D. (2016). Recovery Using the 12 Steps. *Psych Central.* Retrieved on October 1, 2016, from http://psychcentral.com/lib/recovery-using-the-12-steps/

Miller, W. R., & Rose, G. S. (2009). Toward a Theory of Motivational Interviewing. *The American Psychologist, 64*(6), 527–537. http://doi.org/10.1037/a0016830

Rosenberg, K. P., & Feder, L. C. (2014). *Behavioral addictions: criteria, evidence, and treatment.* London ; Waltham, MA: Academic Press.

Sun, A.-P., Ashley, L. L., & Dickson, L. (2012). *Behavioral Addiction: Screening, Assessment, and Treatment.* Las Vegas, NV: Central Recovery Press.

Herkov, M. (2016). About Cognitive Psychotherapy. *Psych Central.* Retrieved on October 1, 2016, from http://psychcentral.com/lib/about-cognitive-psychotherapy/

Psych Central. (2016). An Overview of Dialectical Behavior Therapy. *Psych Central.* Retrieved on October 1, 2016, from http://psychcentral.com/lib/an-overview-of-dialectical-behavior-therapy/

Chapter 7 Resources

This section gives a list of resources for those who wish to seek out more information on the topics presented in the chapter. Complete references appear above.

Printed Resources

The following books/chapters are selections that may help deepen your knowledge of this subject.

Dialectical Behavior Therapy in Clinical Practice: Applications Across Disorders and Settings, Linda Dimeff and Kelly Koerner
Internet Addiction: A Handbook and Guide to Evaluation and Treatment, Young and Nabuco de Abreu
Chapter 9: Psychotherapy for Internet Addiction
Chapter 10: Working with Adolescents Addicted to the Internet
Chapter 13: Toward the Prevention of Adolescent Internet Addiction
Chapter 14: Systemic Dynamics with Adolescents Addicted to the Internet

Online Resources

Addiction.com, Mindfulness as a Treatment for Behavioral Addictions - *https://www.addiction.com/expert-blogs/mindfulness-treatment-behavioral-addictions/*

FDA Safety Alerts - Aripiprazole use in Impulse Control Problems http://www.fda.gov/Safety/MedWatch/SafetyInformation/SafetyAlerts forHumanMedicalProducts/ucm498823.htm?source=govdelivery&utm_me dium=email&utm_source=govdelivery

Beyond Talk: Learning How to Replace Addictive Behaviors Using Cognitive Behavioral Therapy - https://www.promises.com/articles/therapy/replace-addictive-behaviors-cognitive-behavioral-therapy/

Principals of Drug Addiction Treatment - https://www.drugabuse.gov/publications/principles-drug-addiction-treatment-research-based-guide-third-edition/preface

Mindfulness Based Professional Training Center - http://mbpti.org/

Mindfulness Based Relapse Prevention - http://www.mindfulrp.com/default.html

American Addiction Center – Behavioral Addiction Treatment http://americanaddictioncenters.org/behavioral-addictions/

What is Moderation Management - http://www.moderation.org/whatisMM.shtml

In Depth – Cognitive Behavioral Therapy - http://psychcentral.com/lib/in-depth-cognitive-behavioral-therapy/

The Efficacy of Abstinence Treatment Vs. Harm Reduction - https://www.bhpalmbeach.com/recovery-articles/efficacy-abstinence-treatment-vs-harm-reduction

Mindfulness Based Relapse Prevention - http://www.huffingtonpost.com/entry/mindfulness-based-relapse-prevention-interview_us_5645fd24e4b08cda3488638b

Journal Articles

Van Wormer, K. (1999). Harm Induction vs. Harm Reduction: Comparing American and British Approaches to Drug Use. *Journal of Offender Rehabilitation.* 29 (1/2) 35-48. http://www.uni.edu/vanworme/drugpolicy.html

Miller, W. R., & Rose, G. S. (2009). Toward a Theory of Motivational Interviewing. *The American Psychologist, 64*(6), 527–537. http://doi.org/10.1037/a0016830

Bowen S, Witkiewitz K, Clifasefi SL, et al. Relative Efficacy of Mindfulness-Based Relapse Prevention, Standard Relapse Prevention, and Treatment as Usual for Substance Use Disorders: A Randomized Clinical Trial. *JAMA Psychiatry.*2014;71(5):547-556. doi:10.1001/jamapsychiatry.2013.4546.

De Lisle, SM., Dowling, NA., Allen, JS., (2015). Mindfulness-Based Approaches in the Treatment of Disordered Gambling: A Systematic Review and Meta-Analysis. *Research on Social Work Practice.*

De Lisle SM, Dowling NA, Allen JS: Mindfulness and problem gambling: a review of the literature. *Journal of Gambling Studies* 2012. doi:10.1007/s10899–011-9284-7 doi:10.1007/s10899-011-9284-7

Shonin E, Van Gordon W, Griffiths MD: Buddhist philosophy for the treatment of problem gambling. *Journal of Behavioral Addictions* 2013. doi:10.1556/JBA.2.2013.001 doi:10.1556/JBA.2.2013.001

Shonin, Van Gordon, Slade, & Griffiths. (2013). Mindfulness and other Buddhist-derived interventions in correctional settings: A systematic review. *Aggression and Violent Behavior, 18*(3), 365-372.

King, Delfabbro, Griffiths, & Gradisar. (2011). Assessing clinical trials of Internet addiction treatment: A systematic review and CONSORT evaluation. *Clinical Psychology Review, 31*(7), 1110-1116.

King, D., Delfabbro, P., Griffiths, M., & Gradisar, M. (2012). Cognitive-Behavioral Approaches to Outpatient Treatment of Internet Addiction in Children and Adolescents. *Journal of Clinical Psychology, 68*(11), 1185-1195.

Van Gordon, W., Shonin, E., & Griffiths, M. (2015). Towards a second generation of mindfulness-based interventions. *Australian & New Zealand Journal of Psychiatry,49*(7), 591-592.

Pontes, & Griffiths. (2017). The development and psychometric evaluation of the Internet Disorder Scale (IDS-15). *Addictive Behaviors, 64*, 261-268.

Koronczai, B., Kknyei, G., Urbn, R., Kun, B., Ppay, O., Nagygyrgy, K., . . . Demetrovics, Z. (n.d.). The mediating effect of self-esteem, depression and anxiety between satisfaction with body appearance and problematic Internet use. *The American Journal of Drug and Alcohol Abuse, 2013, 2013, Vol.39(4), P.259-265,39*(4), 259-265.

Andreassen, Pallesen, & Griffiths. (2017). The relationship between addictive use of social media, narcissism, and self-esteem: Findings from a large national survey. *Addictive Behaviors, 64*, 287-293.

Kuss, Van Rooij, Shorter, Griffiths, & Van de Mheen. (2013). Internet addiction in adolescents: Prevalence and risk factors. *Computers in Human Behavior, 29*(5), 1987-1996.

Pontes, H., Király, O., Demetrovics, Z., & Griffiths, M. (2014). The conceptualisation and measurement of DSM-5 Internet Gaming Disorder: The development of the IGD-20 Test. *PloS One, 9*(10), E110137.

Griffiths, M. (2012). Internet sex addiction: A review of empirical research. *Addiction Research & Theory, 2012, Vol.20(2), P.111-124, 20*(2), 111-124.

Ryan, & Xenos. (2011). Who uses Facebook? An investigation into the relationship between the Big Five, shyness, narcissism, loneliness, and Facebook usage. *Computers in Human Behavior, 27*(5), 1658-1664.

Aydın, Muyan, & Demir. (2013). The Investigation of Facebook usage Purposes and Shyness, Loneliness. *Procedia - Social and Behavioral Sciences, 93*, 737-741.

Online Videos

Using Cognitive Behavioral Therapy for Treating Addiction
https://www.youtube.com/watch?v=o3tRAduJQAk

Addiction Counseling for Beginners
https://www.youtube.com/watch?v=FHb3AM6NzP0

12-Step Programs for Beginners
https://www.youtube.com/watch?v=PDcqZ4QaVPY

Alcoholics Anonymous – The Basics
https://www.youtube.com/watch?v=N3MIGrvUNgY

Motivational Interviewing for Treatment of Addiction
https://www.youtube.com/watch?v=OWqDRu45vPk

Dr. William Miller on Motivational Interviewing
https://www.youtube.com/watch?v=2yvuem-QYCo

Other Resources

National Institute on Drug Abuse (NIDA), https://www.drugabuse.gov/
National Institute on Alcohol Abuse and Alcoholism (NIAAA), https://www.niaaa.nih.gov/
National Institute of Mental Health (NIMH), https://www.nimh.nih.gov/index.shtml
Center for Substance Abuse Treatment (CSAT), http://www.samhsa.gov/about-us/who-we-are/offices-centers/csat
Substance Abuse and Mental Health Services Administration (SAMHSA), http://www.samhsa.gov/
Anxiety and Depression Association of America (ADAA), https://www.adaa.org/

CHAPTER 8

Prevention and Community Resources for Internet-Based Addictions

Chapter Overview

This chapter is intended to elaborate on the recovery process for Internet addictions. To expand on that concept, we will consider how to prevent and identify these addictions, how to manage them, what relapse looks like, and finally, how to connect clients with important community resources. Again, this section is designed to give the reader only an overview of these concepts; more information on these ideas can be found in the resource guide at the end of the chapter.

Reviewing Key Concepts

This chapter will focus on recovery and relapse prevention. First, however, it is important to emphasize the recovery and relapse prevention depend at the outset on accurate assessment and diagnosis, and these features are still in very early stages of development. Even estimates of prevalence rates range wildly, based on differences in study methodology and the criteria used to determine diagnosis. In general, it is likely that about 6% of Internet users may engage in problematic Internet use, as defined by excessive use and/or the inability to control or curtail its utilization. But Internet technologies are changing rapidly and research has yet to catch up with technology, so prevalence rates are still a moving target as the technologies themselves continue to evolve. Research and clinical practice will need to continue to adapt and adjust to these emerging concerns.

The Internet seems to be a unique platform for addiction for a number of reasons. Unlike substance abuse, there is no direct physiological addiction, but the pleasurable elements of Internet use drive a user to seek out more, and in vulnerable users this can turn to addiction. When considering the accessibility, anonymity, and privacy of typical computer use, it is no surprise that this is a hotbed for dysregulated engagement. Also, the Internet is a platform where individuals can fill other important needs: people may form social connections, find sexual satisfaction, relieve emotions, and feel excitement – all from the comfort of their own homes, or even in places where such activities were previously prohibited such as school classrooms.

Internet addictions can be conceptualized similarly to other forms of behavioral addictions. Addiction as a general disorder has been conceptualized broadly to incorporate the six following elements, with modifications to apply directly to problematic Internet use disorders:

7. *Salience* – The online behavior becomes the most important activity in the person's life and tends to dominate thinking, feeling, and activities.
8. *Mood Modification* – The Internet use has an emotional impact on the individual and serves as both a source of pleasure and a coping strategy.
9. *Tolerance* – Increasing amounts of Internet access are require to achieve the mood-modifying effects, and there is often greater recklessness and destructiveness along with increase in the behavior.
10. *Withdrawal Symptoms* – There are unpleasant feelings or physical impacts when the individual is unable to engage in the behavior.
11. *Conflict* – There are relationship/work/school/responsibility conflicts that arise from excessive engagement online.
12. *Relapse* – Though the individual has attempted to reduce their use, there are repeated reversions to the excessive engagement in the behavior. (Rosenberg & Feder, 2014).

Understanding Internet addictions in this framework helps clinicians unfamiliar with these concerns easily see the potential for harmful effects in the lives of individual clients.

This understanding of addiction comes in part from a more fully developed knowledge of the neurobiological processes that accompany rewarding behaviors. Only recently have we been able to access information on brain processing to a level of detail where neural pathways might be observed (Kimberly S. Young, 2011; Rosenberg & Feder, 2014). Most researchers and clinicians agree that Internet addictions stem from a combination of biological, social, and psychological factors. A number of different biological models for how these disorders develop have been suggested, including the Reward Cycle and cellular memory. Overall, research into the brain chemistry of addiction will continue to develop and reveal information about the form and function of these concerns as more work is done in this area.

Specific attention must be paid to the difficulty of treating Internet addiction. Often questions about Internet use are not a part of a standard intake assessment, and clinicians may not be aware that these issues are present with their clients. Furthermore, the DSM does not formally recognize these disorders which can make diagnosis challenging. However, CBT has been widely used to treat behavioral addictions and other models of substance use treatment are being adapted for use with Internet based disorders. Alternative treatment models are also gaining traction, as mindfulness based practices and yoga are being utilized in treatment. For many behavioral addictions, family therapy is also an extremely important component of recovery (Grant, 2008). Another complicating factor is that unlike substance use disorders, abstinence is likely impossible due to the ubiquitous nature of the Internet in modern society. Though certain websites and behaviors may be avoided, the Internet itself will almost certainly remain part of a client's daily life. Clients and practitioners must work together to create meaningful plans that will help clients find success.

International Responses to Internet Addictions

Because of the worldwide nature of the Internet, these concerns are not limited to the US, though much of the content in this book best applies to US based clinicians. Outside of the US, there has been a considerable increase in discussion around Internet addictions. In many Asian countries, particularly China, Korea, and Singapore, Internet addiction has been identified as a public health threat. Prevalence rates in these countries are considered to be at near-epidemic levels and a bulk of the research in these Internet use disorders comes from these countries. Other European countries, such as Germany and Spain, have active public education and prevention movements and are emphasizing the need for trained clinicians in these areas with a call for professional trainings. The US does not currently have this same level of public awareness or organized prevention and education programs. While this may be in part due to functional differences in Internet access in different countries and cultures, or in part due to a difference in philosophy of health care and preventative care, ultimately the US has some catching up to do in this area.

Overall Goals of Treatment and Education

Overall, the goals of education and treatment for Internet addictions are the following:

1. *Prevention* – Ideally, education and awareness of potentially addictive behaviors paired with instruction in prevention strategies will help at risk populations avoid developing a behavioral addiction. Clinical education will help practitioners to identify vulnerable individuals and educate those individuals on Internet addictions. Increased clinician awareness will also help parents and families create appropriate boundaries around Internet use.

2. *Identifying the Problem* – When a behavior has progressed to a clinically significant level, clinicians will identify the concern and begin appropriate treatment. Again, most Internet addictions do not have an empirically supported, specific treatment model; however, modifications to traditional addiction treatments can be made to treat these concerns effectively.

3. *Managing the Addiction* – Though no specific ongoing recommendations exist for Internet use and Internet addiction, an integrative and individualized strategy for treatment will be utilized to help clients manage their addictive behaviors. Clients at this stage will work towards limiting the repetitive thoughts, actions or behaviors and instead using the Internet in the ways that are not "excessive". Again, time is not the only consideration as Internet connection becomes nearly constant in our society.

4. *Relapse Prevention* – As a client comes in control of their addiction, they should be encouraged with positive reinforcement and continued treatment for comorbid concerns. This is a continued process.

5. *Recovery* – The client changes or completely stops the behavior and is in control of their level of engagement. Clients and practitioners should work together to define what successful recovery looks like for each individual.

Preventing Internet Addictions

Because the Internet is becoming a ubiquitous part of everyday life, it is likely that we will see a rise in problematic Internet use in the future. With this prediction comes motivation to work towards strategies that can predict and prevent these concerns. Firstly, monitoring at risk individuals for early engagement in Internet addictions may help catch these behaviors before they progress to clinically significant levels. This is particularly important for parents as children and adolescents are fast becoming consumers of online media. To this end, the high comorbidity rates of Internet addictions may be a blessing, as many of these clients may already be in treatment for other concerns and well educated practitioners may be able to notice the early signs of concerning engagement in an addictive behavior. As previously noted, questions about Internet use should be added to intake assessments, especially for those working with at risk populations. Genetic and neurobiological research may help to identify vulnerable individuals before addictions occur, and continued clinical observation may assist with building a better sense of the demographics that struggle most with problematic usage. Additionally, general increased education on coping may help to prevent the development of these addictions as maladaptive coping strategies.

In preventing Internet addictions, teaching reasonable use and moderation are key. This knowledge based and educational approach is based in part on the assumption that Internet addictions occur due to lack of knowledge about the potential consequences as compared to substance use disorders (Kimberly S. Young, 2011). Because college students and adolescents are often the impacted population with certain Internet addictions, specific education strategies addressed to this population may also prove useful. However, other populations are at risk for these addictions as well, and there may be different profiles for each subset of Internet addiction. Careful clinical consideration and additional research is needed to understand more about these issues.

Additionally, understanding what attracts individuals to the Internet may inspire preventative measures that get at the core of the problem. Attraction to the Internet stems from a complicated compilation of factors that can be summarized into the following list: 1. Content factors, 2. Accessibility Factors, 3. Reinforcement Factors 4. Social Factors and 5. Generational Factors (Young, 2011). Understanding these factors and their impacts may help aid in prevention of problematic Internet use. Content factors refers to the highly stimulating content available online – from sexual content, videos, computer gaming, financial information and news, shopping, sports, music and more. There are few things one could be interested in and not find information about online and much of the available content is inherently fun and desirable.

Accessibility factors involve the individual's ability to control their online experience and access this control whenever they want. With increasing Internet speeds, there is hardly any delay between desire and access, and with the disinhibiting and anonymous elements of the Internet, this creates a sort of perfect storm for addiction.

Furthermore, the variable reinforcement schedule of the Internet increases the compelling nature of Internet use (Young, 2011). Even a seemingly mundane online task – checking one's email – occurs in this highly reinforcing pattern: you never know when an email is going to be received, who it is from, or what it contains. Variable reinforcement schedules are known for having the most extinction resistance, an important note for those working to treat Internet additions. The Internet also has a social element that drives people towards use. The Internet is both socially connecting and isolating and offers a level of control around social interaction that is not typically found in in-person exchanges. For those with low social skills, there is ample opportunity to find connection online that may not be as easy to manage in "real life." Finally, generational differences may be a part of the appeal of the Internet. Today's children, adolescents and young adults have been largely raised with access to the Internet and this group is generally highly adept at using computer technologies. This creates confusion in family structures, as the undereducated adults struggle to create appropriate rules around Internet use because they do not understand the technology as well as their children.

Preventive Measures

Internet addiction can be harmful if left unresolved and untreated. Preventive measures have to be implemented as soon as possible to mitigate the problem. There are many preventative measures to avoid Internet addiction.

Studies suggest that Internet addiction often starts because of the lack of real-life social support. Thus, people whose lifestyle involves spending too much time being alone like homemakers, singles, retired and the disabled are often at risk of developing Internet addiction.

Other situations that may give rise to Internet addiction include big and dramatic life changes such as loss of a job, divorce, breakup and death of loved ones. While these situations are hard to avoid, it is crucial that you learn how to deal with these Internet addiction traps. Below are the things that you can do to prevent Internet addiction even before it starts.

- **Get a hobby that does not involve the Internet or computers:** Getting involved with real hobbies that are not related to the Internet or computers can take your mind off the Internet. Reconnect with yourself and do the things that you used to love. You can join local clubs in your area that support your hobbies so that you can also meet new people.

- **Help with household chores:** Instead of spending time online, parents should encourage their children to help with the household chores. This will also teach children important life skills like organizing and cooking. Aside from keeping children off the computer, it will also increase their confidence in life.

- **Improve real networking:** Hanging out with friends is a great way to improve meaningful social networking. There are many ways to hang out with friends but make sure you avoid places that have free Internet access.

- **Use the public computer:** If you want to control your Internet use, you can opt to use the public computer or the library computer especially when you are looking up information. This will force you to use the computer or the Internet at a limited time thus controlling your compulsion.

- **Limit your computer time:** The best way to prevent Internet addiction is to limit computer use. Set a date at least once a week to unplug from your computer, laptop, smart phone or tablet. Make it as a conscious effort to not use it on the scheduled day.

- **Don't use your gadgets when doing chores and other things:** Whether you are taking a bath, eating your dinner or doing other things, never bring your computer or gadgets with you otherwise you will be tempted to go online.

- **Treat the underlying causes:** There are many reasons why people suffer from Internet addiction. Most of these reasons include depression, anxiety and stress. If you suffer from any of these afflictions, getting yourself treated can decrease your chances of falling into Internet addiction. Before your Internet habit becomes part of your mechanism to escape from stress or depression, reach out to a close friend or therapist who can help with your psychological problems before it leads to Internet addiction.

- **Build your support network:** Creating a solid support network can help you from falling victim to Internet addiction. A good support network can provide outlet for stress and can help you have an active social life. Remember that psychological dilemmas always go together with Internet addiction, thus opening yourself to real interactions can help reduce your risk of becoming susceptible.

- **Community-based prevention program:** Schools and communities should establish prevention programs that do not only involve the participation of students, teachers and parents but practically all stakeholders within the community. This type of program is necessary to promote public awareness of the serious effects of Internet addiction and how it affects the society as a whole.
- **Youth development programs:** Youth development programs provide young people, who are addicted to the Internet, a promising direction in their future. This kind of program often results in young people showing higher levels of psychosocial competencies and less problematic behavior. It also reduces their risk by improving their inner strengths so that they can co-exist with the Internet without falling victim to addiction.
- **Inter-agency strategies:** The media plays a very important role in the rise of Internet addiction. Inter-agency strategies encourage different agencies to develop strategies to prevent Internet addiction. This strategy requires immense effort from government agencies and private groups to reduce Internet addiction. Examples of strategies may include regulating websites that can potential cause Internet addiction and promote public awareness.
- **Get a virtual assistant:** If you work online and you suffer from Internet addiction, you can get a virtual assistant so that you won't have to spend too much time online. Virtual assistants' service fees are fairly inexpensive and they can work on an hourly rate. This is a great way to limit your access to the Internet until you have completely dealt with your addiction successfully.
- **Don't use the Internet for recreational purposes:** Most people go to the Internet to be entertained. To prevent Internet addiction, remove Internet use as one of your recreational incentives. Instead, only use it for business. To do this, uninstall computer games and stay away from social networking sites to remove your urge from using the Internet. Instead, look for recreational activities in real life so that you can replace the Internet with them as a form of entertainment.
- **Track your progress:** Always remind yourself of your progress by tracking the amount of time that you spend on the Internet. Compare the time that you have spent online to the boundaries that you have set in the first place. If your progress indicates that you are doing a good job, reward yourself.
- **Do digital dieting:** Digital dieting refers to reducing the amount of time that you spend on the Internet. This strategy was developed by Dr. Kimberly Young and it includes three principles (1) checking

your Internet habits, (2) setting time limits and (3) disconnecting to reconnect to reality. Under this strategy, Dr. Kimberly suggests that people should reduce the amount of times to check your devices for updates and messages, regulating the Internet usage to prevent excessive Internet use, and do digital detox for at least 48 hours.[8]

Identifying Problematic Internet Behavior

As discussed previously in this resource guide, identifying Internet addictions may be uniquely challenging as use of the Internet is required for many facets of daily life and there is a blurred line between recreational and pathological use. A key element in deciding should be identifying the consequences of the behavior, the user's own attitudes and previous attempts at reducing their use, and also what the client experiences when they attempt to reduce use. Many of the abstinence based, 12-step programs emphasize the loss of control and unmanageability of the behavior when trying to define when an excessive behavior has crossed the line into addiction (Rosenberg & Feder, 2014). While healthy enthusiasms add to life, behavioral addictions take away from it, even though momentary pleasure may be felt when engaging in the behavior. Furthermore, those with Internet addictions are partially motivated by the drive to reduce the mounting tension they feel around the compulsion to engage in the behavior rather than for pleasure alone.

Though focusing on substance addictions, these signs of addiction from the National Council on Alcoholism and Drug Dependence may be useful for clinicians helping patients who may have an Internet addiction. The signs are as follows, with modifications to the language for Internet based addictions:

1. *Loss of Control*: Engaging in online activity more than a person wants to, for longer than they intended, or despite telling themselves that they wouldn't do it this time.
2. *Neglecting Other Activities*: Spending less time on activities that used to be important (hanging out with family and friends, exercising, pursuing hobbies or other interests) because of their time online; drop in attendance and performance at work or school.
3. *Risk Taking*: More likely to take serious risks in order to engage in the activity of choice. Making unsafe decisions online despite knowledge of potential consequences
4. *Relationship Issues*: People struggling with addiction are known to act out against those closest to them, particularly if someone is

attempting to address their addiction-related problems; complaints from co-workers, supervisors, teachers or classmates.

5. *Secrecy*: Going out of one's way to hide the amount of engagement in online activities or one's actions surrounding the addiction. People with Internet addictions may also be excessively or ritualistically protective over access to their computer in an attempt to hide their online activities.

6. *Changing Appearance*: Serious changes or deterioration in hygiene or physical appearance – lack of showering, slovenly appearance, unclean clothes. Internet addicts may also present with serious sleep deprivation. In other cases, with some cyber relational or cyber sexual addictions, appearance may change drastically in an attempt to please a new online connection.

7. *Family History*: A family history of addiction can increase one's vulnerability to behavioral addictions

8. *Tolerance*: Over time, a person adapts their online activity to the point that they need more and more of it in order to have the same reaction, or in the case of cybersexual addictions, this may be represented in an increase in the intensity of content viewed.

9. *Withdrawal*: As mood modifying impacts of the Internet use wear off the person may experience psychological symptoms of withdrawal and may have intense feelings of distress when not able to access the Internet.

10. *Continued Use Despite Negative Consequences:* Even though it is causing problems (on the job, in relationships, for one's health), a person continues engaging in the behavior. ("Signs and Symptoms of Addiction," 2015).

Using this list of concerns may help to differentiate between normative behaviors and addictive patterns.

Though clinicians have a part in identifying potential Internet addictions based on clinical interview, client observation and refined judgement, a client may be resistant to discussing their behaviors. They may be unaware that what they are struggling with is something that should be discussed in a mental health setting, fear legal or interpersonal repercussions or even reject the concept that they are an "Addict" because of the stigma associated with this term. Increased awareness about these concerns should help to allow clients to seek out help and also educate clinicians about why some clients may be resistant to treatment.

Managing Internet Addictions

After identifying an issue with Internet use, a practitioner should work together with a client and their family (when necessary) to create a management plan to reduce the negative consequences of the behavior. Currently, as no specific therapeutic interventions are suggested, treatment tends to be individualized to match a client's concerns (Rosenberg & Feder, 2014). In some cases, this might be a plan based in part on abstinence. For example, some clients may choose to prevent themselves from accessing sexual content online through a firewall or may remove accounts and access to online games. For some clients, modification of the behavior will be more reasonable. For example, for a client who compulsively shops online, a budget could be made and credit limits lowered to reduce spending potential, and the clinician could teach mindfulness techniques to manage urges. Overall, day to day management of Internet addictions and effective clinical intervention are inherently integrative. A number of studies have demonstrated the role that negative affect and mood modification play in development of addictions, therefore, one strategy for managing these addictions may be to intervene in habits around affect regulation (Grant, 2008; Rosenberg & Feder, 2014).

Relapse

Relapse is a natural part of the recovery process. In many cases, relapse is an opportunity to learn more about what might be causing particular behaviors as well as process triggers and identify the role of affect and mood. Though relapse is natural, it is also natural to want to prevent relapse such that a patient can have more control over the consequences of their online behaviors. Again, much of the discussion around relapse comes from literature on substance abuse, but can be modified to fit the criteria and unique concerns of Internet addictions.

Terence Gorski wrote extensively about relapse prevention in his 1986 book, Staying Sober: A Guide for Relapse Prevention. He developed the list after working with chronically relapsing patients with alcohol addictions (see below). For ease of use, the list of warning signs of relapse is available as a pamphlet that can be printed and then carried in a purse or briefcase. This is a great resource for both patients and practitioners! Gorski suggests that relapse is a process, not an isolated event, and as such, when a client and clinician are aware of the warning signs, the process can be interrupted. The phases and warning signs of relapse are as follows:

1. Getting Stuck in Recovery
2. Denying that We're Stuck
3. Using Other Compulsions
4. Experiencing a Trigger Event
5. Becoming Dysfunctional on the Inside
6. Becoming Dysfunctional on the Outside
7. Losing Control
8. Using Addictive Thinking
9. Engaging in Addictive Behaviors

Gorski categorizes these steps into three broad categories: 1. Emotional Relapse, 2. Mental Relapse, and 3. Physical Relapse. In emotional relapse, an addict is not thinking of returning to previous behaviors, but rather not properly managing their emotions which may set the stage for relapse. Mental relapse is a return of ambivalence around using and finally, physical relapse is return to inappropriate and consequential online activities.

In order to help prevent relapse, practitioners should encourage their patients to be honest about their ambivalence rather than attempt to "do well" in therapy. Clients may feel concerned about sharing the desire to re-engage in behaviors because they worry they will be judged for returning to maladaptive patterns, especially if they are feeling shame around the content of their Internet use (as is often the case in cyber-sexual addictions. Mindfulness Based Relapse Prevention has been shown to be effective in helping clients avoid relapse (Rosenberg & Feder, 2014). Other relaxation and replacement behaviors can also be taught to clients to help them manage their emotions and mitigate their desire to use the Internet as a mechanism to mood management.

Support Groups

Support groups are effective in bringing Internet addicts together so that they can face the same issues and make major changes in their lives. Support groups allow their members to share advices and experiences so that they can be helpful to those who are still struggling with their addiction.

Unlike other support groups for other types of addiction, Internet addiction support groups are new. Most rehabilitation centers that offer treatments for Internet addiction also provide support groups to their patients. However, some people have established support groups to fill the need of many Internet addicts and families who are searching for support groups within their areas.

Joining support groups is helpful for those who needs support beyond what their family and friends can offer. The best thing about support groups is that it allows members to relate to one another through their experiences thus they get the feeling that they are not alone in facing their problems.

What Is a Support Group?

A support group is when people, who share the same concern, gather. In this case, Internet addicts meet other people who also suffer the same Internet compulsions. Contrary to common belief, support groups are not similar to group therapy sessions. While the latter is a formal type of treatment done within a group setting and led by a trained therapist, support groups are formed by anyone who is interested in reaching out to others who suffer from the same Internet addiction condition.

Internet addiction support group sessions are often done in person wherein professional facilitators like a social worker, psychologist or a nurse oversee the entire activity. Activities can range from educational to discussion depending on the support group's vision.

The premise of addiction support groups is to help patients address their maladaptive cognitions that have led to negative feelings while helping them build real-life relationships with other people so that they can release their inhibitions as well as the excessive need to use the Internet.

Benefits of Joining Support Groups

Internet addicts can get significant benefit from joining support groups. Regardless of the format used, joining support groups is a great way for Internet addicts to meet people who share the same problems as them. Support groups that are tailored to the life situation of patients can help improve their ability to make new friends so that they can work together to decrease their dependencies on the Internet. The benefits of support groups are as follows:

- Feeling empowered and in control of one's compulsions
- Feeling less isolated and lonely
- Able to form new friendship from people who suffer from the same condition
- Becomes interactive during group discussion
- Being able to talk with honesty about your feelings
- Improving your coping mechanisms as well as your ability to adjust to new situations

- Developing a clear understanding on what to expect with different random and overwhelming situations
- Reducing depression, stress and anxiety
- Getting useful and practical advice about different treatments
- Getting updated resources such as therapist information and other treatment options

Since Internet addiction exists in different forms, patients can look for support groups that fit their situation. For instance, if a patient suffers Internet addiction because he or she is suffering from loneliness and anxiety, he or she may join a singles group to meet new people.

How to Find Internet Addiction Support Groups

There are different types of support groups designed for people who suffer from Internet addiction. To fully recover from an addiction, it is not enough to join an Internet addiction support group randomly. Finding the right group can be key to recovery. Here are some tips that can be useful to provide to patients struggling with an Internet addiction who may be interested in finding suitable support groups.

- **Ask your health care provider:** Ask your doctor, therapist or psychologist to recommend a support group for your Internet addiction problem.
- **Check local listings:** Find a support group by checking your local listing.
- **Look online:** Ask a family member or friend to help you look for a support group online. However, it is advisable that you don't opt for an online support group format because you need to decrease your dependency on the Internet. Looking online for support groups means that you need to collect the necessary information of an Internet addiction support group within your area. Once you find a support group, attend the meeting in person.
- **Contact community centers:** Ask community centers like churches, libraries and temples in your area if they know about the existence of support groups within your area.
- **Contact organizations:** Contact organizations that are devoted to your condition. For instance, the Center for Internet Addiction founded by Dr. Kimberly Young in 1995 is a useful resources for Internet addiction.

There is an increasing number of Internet addiction support groups that have been established to cater to the rising number of Internet addicts who are looking for support groups where they can share their experiences and meet with people they share the same experiences with.

What to Ask Before Joining an Internet Addiction Support Group

Before joining a support group, it is important to ask the right questions.[9] Below are the things to ask before joining a support group.

- Is it dedicated towards a specific Internet compulsion?
- When is the meeting schedule?
- Is the location convenient?
- Who is the moderator or facilitator of the meeting?
- Will there be an expert present during the group discussion?
- Will my condition be kept confidential?
- What is the meeting usually like?
- Does the group follow established ground rules?
- Does it meet my cultural needs?
- Is it free? If not, then how much is the fee?

When choosing a support group for Internet addiction, it is important that the format and environment are comfortable.. Members in support groups come and go so it is crucial to evaluate the group regularly if it continues to meet its stipulated needs.

In addition, people change over time in support groups, as in life. What might represent a good fit at one stage of recovery may not be ideal for another. It is important to remain open to regularly re-assessing the value of the group, and the possibility of changing it if need be.

Internet Addiction Support Group Red Flags

Since not all support groups may be a good match for your clients' needs, there are certain red flags that are helpful to know. Below are the red flags that signal problems when joining a particular Internet addiction support group:

- Guarantees a cure for your Internet addiction
- Group leaders urge you to stop other treatments that you are taking
- Imposes high fees before you can join the session
- Pressures you to purchase their products and services

- Encourage members to be disruptive during the session
- Gives judgment of your actions and decisions

If a particular Internet addiction support group is raises no red flags, then it's worth joining the sessions.. To be able to get the most out of a support group, simply listen at first, especially if for anyone who may be shy or reserved. As comfort levels build, active participation can begin, sharing thoughts and ideas and experiences.

Internet Addiction Support Groups

Support groups for Internet addiction provide avenues for Internet addicts to meet other people who share the same situation. Below are the different types of support groups that are available to help Internet addicts.

- <u>Internet and Technology Addiction Anonymous (ITAA)</u>: This is support group that is geared towards people who are dealing with excessive Internet use. Aside from working with patients, ITAA also provides session with family members of Internet addicts. The support group offers resources to people who are suffering from social, interpersonal and economic problems caused by excessive Internet use.
- <u>Internet Addiction Support Group</u>: With more than 19,000 members and still growing, this support group provides support not only to Internet addicts but also to their family and friends.
- <u>Gaming and Internet Addiction Group</u>: This support group is located in Temecula, California and it focuses on patients who suffer from gaming and Internet addictions. People who suffer from online gambling can also join this support group. The group has face to face meetings. You can ask for the schedule from the link provided.
- <u>University Of Michigan's Internet Addiction Support Group</u>: This online Internet addiction support group was founded in 2004 to help students who suffer from Internet addiction. It also welcomes non-student members. This Internet addiction support group provides a venue for people to express their feelings about Internet addiction. The group is sponsored by the Center for Internet Addiction Recovery.
- <u>Internet Addicts of the Bay Area Support Group</u>: This Internet addiction support group provide support to Internet addicts located in the Bay Area. It is designed to help locals provide support to one

another. The group is modeled after the 12 steps and it does not require any fees for members to join.

Internet Addiction Resources

Individuals who are well-informed about their conditions make faster progress in terms of their recovery. This Internet addiction resource includes articles on various topics about Internet addiction that your clients might find find useful.

- <u>Net Addictions FAQs</u>: Learn what Internet addiction is, its causes, diagnosis, treatment and prevention at the best resource for the topic. This website will let you understand what you need to know about Internet addiction.
- <u>Google Scholar</u>: Look for published articles related to Internet addiction. Free articles are available in this site that covers the causes of Internet addiction, prevention as well as other topics related to it.
- <u>Online Addiction Quiz</u>: Take a self-test check to find out whether you are suffering from Internet addiction or if you are at a high risk of developing this compulsive addiction.
- <u>Self-Test</u>: Doing self-test to validate Internet addiction is provided by this website. You can take a lot of self-test check if you suspect yourself suffering from Internet addiction.
- <u>Psychiatry Online – Issues for DSM-5: Internet Addiction</u>: This is the published report of Internet addiction as part of the compulsive-impulsive spectrum disorder that involves both offline and online computer use.
- <u>Psych Centrals' Internet Addiction Resources</u>: This website has a listing of Internet resources and other related topics.
- <u>Center for Online Addiction</u>: Established by Dr. Kimberly Young, one of the pioneers in the study of Internet addiction, the Center for Online Addiction offers books and workshops for professional therapists who want to improve their skills in treating this disorder.
- <u>Common Sense Media</u>: This website provides resources on how to prevent Internet addiction to children. It is a great website for parents who want to curb the excessive Internet use of their children.
- <u>Internet Addiction – Tips for Parents</u>: Another useful website for parents, this site allows parents to explore practice advice on how to deal with Internet addiction among teenagers and children.

Internet addiction might be a new type of addiction but with many people suffering from it and their numbers increasing, there is no wonder why concerns around it are increasing, as well. While the Internet is becoming a ubiquitous tool to search for information and communicate with other people, there is still a way to deal with excessive Internet use.

Connecting Clients with Resources

Knowing resources for clients can help connect them with support networks outside of individual session. Here are some general resources for clients.

National Institute on Drug Abuse (NIDA), https://www.drugabuse.gov/

National Institute on Alcohol Abuse and Alcoholism (NIAAA), https://www.niaaa.nih.gov/

National Institute of Mental Health (NIMH), https://www.nimh.nih.gov/index.shtml

Center for Substance Abuse Treatment (CSAT), http://www.samhsa.gov/about-us/who-we-are/offices-centers/csat

Substance Abuse and Mental Health Services Administration (SAMHSA), http://www.samhsa.gov/

Anxiety and Depression Association of America (ADAA), https://www.adaa.org/

Psychology Today - http://www.psycholoytoday.com

National Council on Problem Gambling (NCPG) - http://www.ncpgambling.org

National Council for Behavioral Health - http://www.thenationalcouncil.org

Recovery.org - http://www.recovery.org/browse/phoenix-az/

References

Grant, J. E. (2008). *Impulse control disorders: a clinician's guide to understanding and treating behavioral addictions* (1st ed.). New York: W.W. Norton.

Kimberly S. Young, C. N. d. A. (Ed.) (2011). *Internet Addition: A Handbook and Guide to Evaluation and Treatment.* Hoboken, NJ: John Wiley & Sons Inc. .

Rosenberg, K. P., & Feder, L. C. (2014). *Behavioral addictions: criteria, evidence, and treatment.* London ; Waltham, MA: Academic Press.

Signs and Symptoms of Addiction. (2015, 25 July 2015). Retrieved from https://www.ncadd.org/about-addiction/signs-and-symptoms/signs-and-symptoms